THE LAST COMMUNARD

THE LAST COMMUNARD

Adrien Lejeune, the Unexpected
Life of a Revolutionary

GAVIN BOWD

VERSO
London • New York

First published by Verso 2016

1 3 5 7 9 10 8 6 4 2

Verso
UK: 6 Meard Street, London W1F 0EG
US: 20 Jay Street, Suite 1010, Brooklyn, NY 11201
versobooks.com

Verso is the imprint of New Left Books

ISBN-13: 978-1-78478-285-6
ISBN-13: 978-1-78478-288-7 (US EBK)
ISBN-13: 978-1-78478-287-0 (UK EBK)

British Library Cataloguing in Publication Data
A catalogue record for this book is available from the British Library

Library of Congress Cataloging-in-Publication Data

Names: Bowd, Gavin, 1966– author.
Title: The last communard / Gavin Bowd.
Other titles: Dernier communard. English
Description: [First edition] | Brooklyn, NY : Verso,
[2016] | Includes
  bibliographical references and index.
Identifiers: LCCN 2016007024 | ISBN
9781784782856 (hardback : alk. paper)
Subjects: LCSH: Lejeune, Adrien, 1847–1942. |
  Revolutionaries – France – Biography. | Communists
– France – Biography. |
  French – Soviet Union – Biography. | Paris (France)
– History – Commune, 1871.
Classification: LCC DC342.8.L384 B6913 2016 | DDC
335.43092 – dc23
LC record available at http://lccn.loc.gov/2016007024

Typeset in in Fournier by MJ & N Gavan, Truro, Cornwall
Printed in the US by Maple Press

Whoever creates for the people false revolutionary legends, who amuses them with enchanting stories, is as criminal as the geographer who makes untruthful maps for navigators.

Prosper-Olivier Lissagaray

Property is theft.

Pierre-Joseph Proudhon

Contents

Introduction

From One Wall to Another

On 10 November 1989, the day after the fall of the Berlin Wall, I discovered the last Communard. Having been a young communist for a decade, I tried to clear my head of the cataclysmic news of the previous day and repaired to one of my favourite places for solitary contemplation in Paris, the cemetery of Père-Lachaise. Here I wandered among dead leaves and neglected tombs, until I arrived at the corner in the south-east of the cemetery called Le Mur des Fédérés.

Here the very atmosphere of the place distinguishes it from the rest of the necropolis. It is a realm of memory, layered with several periods of history. It was in front of this wall, legend has it, that the Paris Commune ended, when on 28 May 1871, 147 of its citizen's militia, known as Fédérés (after the Federation of the National Guard), were shot before being hastily buried in a shallow grave. This massacre was represented soon after in Ernest Pichio's apocalyptic painting *Le triomphe de l'ordre*, which depicts young and old, women and children, being mown down and tumbling into an abyss. Indeed, the place became a shrine to what was seen as a tragic experiment in

Ernest Pichio, *Le triomphe de l'ordre* (1875)

people's democracy. Facing the wall, which now boasts a commemorative plaque, are several relatively discreet monuments to the survivors of that bloody episode: the tombs of Jean-Baptiste Clément, author of the song 'Le Temps des cerises' in which cherries are compared to drops of blood lies here, as well as Paul Lafargue, husband of Laura Marx, with whom he committed suicide in 1911 to escape the impairment of old age.

In this section of the cemetery, I wandered along the great circular avenue that held many Communist graves, where, until very recently, the French Communist Party (PCF), buried almost all its dignitaries: the 'Son of the People' Maurice Thorez; the clandestine party leader of the Second World War, Jacques Duclos; the founding leader Marcel Cachin; the *L'Humanité* editor Paul Vaillant-Couturier; and the writers Henri Barbusse and Paul Eluard. Beside the grave of Duclos, I noticed for the first time a small black tombstone. It bore a simple epitaph:

Adrien Lejeune, the last Communard, died in Novosibirsk; USSR; 1942

I stood for a few minutes in front of this modest grave and wondered about the things he might have seen in such a long life. What was he doing in the USSR in the darkest days of the Second World War? How did he find his way back to this corner of Paris, to rest in front of the wall where the last Communards fell?

In the weeks and months afterwards these questions continued to nag at me, and, despite the historic upheavals that were occurring around the world, curiosity kept bringing me back to the name engraved on that little black stone. And I started to see what I could find out about this enigma.

L'Humanité, the official paper of the PCF, was my first port of call. On 22 May 1971 – the centenary year of the Paris Commune – the front page of the broadsheet had displayed a photograph of Lejeune over an article entitled 'One hundred years on. The Communard Lejeune will rest near his last barricade':

Yesterday at Le Bourget, the regular Aeroflot Moscow–Paris flight brought back the ashes of Alfred [*sic*] Lejeune, the last of the Communards, who died aged ninety-five in 1942 in Novosibirsk (Soviet Union). The urn was carried by the president of the Party Committee of Novosibirsk, Filatov, accompanied by the academician Inozentsev of the Central Committee of the Communist Party of the Soviet Union and by comrade Pankov, collaborator at the Central Committee. They were greeted by Gaston Plissonnier and Paul Laurent of the Political Bureau of the French Communist Party, Lucien Mathey of the Central Committee, secretary of the Federation of Seine-Saint-Denis, Jean Braire, general secretary of the 'Friends of the Commune', Maurice Niles, deputy-mayor of Drancy, the secretary of the communist cell of the Airport of Le Bourget, etc. Accompanying the representatives of the embassy of the USSR was a delegation from Bagnolet, led by our comrade Joineau, deputy-mayor. It is in the *mairie* of Bagnolet, his home town, that the ashes of Alfred Lejeune have been displayed. A ceremony will take place there tomorrow morning at ten with the participation of the Soviet delegation and Jacques Duclos. Already yesterday afternoon the local population began to pay their respects to the urn. The urn will be transported on Sunday to the Mur des Fédérés where a last homage will be paid to Alfred Lejeune by all the participants in the Centenary Demonstration.

On page five, Fernand Chatel recounted the story of this great survivor, this time managing to spell his name correctly. Adrien Lejeune, we learn, was born on 3 June 1847, in Bagnolet. His father was a barrel-maker, his mother a seamstress. He was forced to earn his living from a young age at a variety of jobs. After many nights and Sundays spent studying, he became a herbalist in a pharmacy. Two years later, aged twenty-two, Adrien Lejeune joined the Republican Association of Freethinkers that brought together socialists and progressives in opposition to the imperial regime and its staunch ally, the Catholic Church. Though protest marches were forbidden, the funeral of each freethinker turned into a popular demonstration against the Empire and oppression. In February 1870, at the close of one such funeral procession in Bagnolet, Adrien Lejeune addressed the crowd. On 4 September 1870, after Emperor Napoleon III's declaration of war against Prussia had led to disaster at Sedan and his own capture, an uprising in Paris culminated in the proclamation of the Third Republic.

Although, for health reasons, Lejeune was unfit to serve in the army, he joined the National Guard to fight against the siege of Paris by Otto von Bismarck's troops. He was a sergeant in the 2nd Company of the 28th Battalion. On 18 March 1871, Lejeune 'did not hesitate for an instant' and went up the Butte de Montmartre, the hill dominating northern Paris, to defend the cannon of the National Guard. He was therefore among those who proclaimed the Commune that same day. During those feverish weeks, Adrien Lejeune divided his time between Bagnolet and the *mairie* of the 20th arrondissement, a Communard hotbed. When the troops of the government based in Versailles invaded the capital, he fought bravely. 'We defended one barricade after another', Lejeune would later write. 'Thus I reached the barricade in the rue des Pyrénées in the district of Belleville. It was the night of 27 to 28 May. And in the morning they caught me'. He was recognised and arrested while trying to reach the *mairie* of the 20th arrondissement. On 12 February 1872 he was sentenced to five years' detention in a floating prison. He helped his comrades to escape. He was later sent to the labour camp at Nouméa (New Caledonia, in the south Pacific), until in 1880, with the general amnesty, he returned to Bagnolet.

In 1905, after following the movement of Communard leader Edouard Vaillant, he joined Jean Jaurès and Jules Guesde in the Unified Socialist Party. In 1917 he 'greeted with enthusiasm the socialist October Revolution which meant the triumph of the Commune's ideas in one sixth of the globe'. In 1922, now aged seventy-five, the old Communard joined the young French Communist Party. Despite age and illness, his mind was 'still combative', which meant more run-ins with the police of the reactionary government. An international committee, specifically created to help the survivors of the Commune, arranged for him to take refuge in the Soviet Union. In 1926, Adrien Lejeune left France for what he would describe as his 'second country'. On the eve of his departure, he gave Marcel Cachin, director of *L'Humanité*, all his savings and his shares in the newspaper. In Moscow, Lejeune lived in the House of the Veterans of the Revolution. In 1936, he donated his meagre savings to the children of Spanish Republicans killed in the struggle against Franco. In October 1941, as Hitler's troops approached Moscow, Adrien Lejeune, with the schoolchildren and old people of his district, was evacuated to Novosibirsk, in Siberia. Fernand Chatel concluded:

There was a ration card for everyone except for the last living Communard, whose rallying cries were read out in the units of the Red Army. His last letter, on 31 December 1941, wished a Happy New Year to the Red Army wounded being treated at the hospital of Novosibirsk. He died on 9 January 1942, at the age of ninety-five, in that Siberian city which still has a street named after him and where not a day goes by without some flowers being laid upon his grave.[1]

L'Humanité's account presented Lejeune as the embodiment of the perfect Communard: of modest origins but with a ferocious appetite for self-education, a freethinker, active in all the uprisings and on all the barricades, present to the bitter end. Afterwards he paid the price for his beliefs – labour camp and deportation – alongside his fellow Communards. However, his commitment never wavered and he became an early adherent to French Marxism, rallying to the Third International before finding a second homeland, the USSR. It was only fitting that such a hero should be given a garlanded return to this historic burial ground on such an anniversary. His reinterment symbolised the very act of memorialisation, while his life and death epitomised the hopes and brutal realities of the revolutionary movement itself.

The newspaper report increased my interest in Lejeune, yet I was aware that this could hardly be the complete story. Where did the truth lie within the mythologising pages of *L'Humanité*? I soon discovered that the facts were elusive and impossible to reconstruct in their entirety. My research in the archives of the Comintern in Moscow, and the French Communist Party in Bobigny, as well as in those of the Historical Service of the Ministry of Defence, at the Château de Vincennes, revealed a considerable gap between the last Communard's life and his legend – a legend in which Adrien Lejeune himself was complicit.

By excavating the records and getting as close as possible to the real man, I realised how history can be made from the least likely participants. The story of Lejeune is not just the history of the last Communard, but a model of how history itself is made. This humble man became a measure of the fall and rise and fall of communism in Europe in the century since he first stood on the barricades. The way his life and story have been appropriated, sold and retold is as important as the action he took on the streets in 1871.

1

Birth of a Communard

On the evening of 3 June 1847, Adrien Félix Lejeune was born at home in the small village of Bagnolet. His parents had been married since 1834, and he had one brother. At the time of Lejeune's birth, this hamlet at the gates of Paris, a mere three miles from the centre of the capital, was growing rapidly: in the twenty-one years from 1851 to 1872, it doubled in size to 2,597 people. The inhabitants still cultivated their plots, growing redcurrants and blackcurrants, raspberries, lilacs and fruit trees. It was essentially a rural population that benefitted from the expansion of the capital nearby. The 'factories' were still workshops that produced, in artisan fashion, varnishes, boxes, glues and leathers; but they also produced, in the melting-pots of exploitation, the proletariat. Clearly, the future Communard was of modest origins, but from a milieu still far from that associated with the Bagnolet that would, in the next century, become a citadel of the 'Red Belt', the ring of staunchly Communist municipalities surrounding Paris.

In a special issue of *France-URSS*, organ of the France-USSR friendship society, published to mark the centenary of the Commune, René Duchet wrote of how Adrien's father had been one of those proletarians, and how the child was obliged to work for a living. He goes on to speculate that the boy nevertheless had ambition, courage and tenacity: he spent all his spare time reading and studying. At the age of twenty, Duchet confirms, he managed to get taken on in a pharmacy as a herbalist. He 'suffered from the injustice and poverty that the people around him suffered'.[1] Many accounts of Lejeune's life use this narrative of self-discovery and liberation, which leads, in inexorably linear fashion, from modest origins through proletarianisation to the scientific communism of the future. As we shall see, such narratives could be rather selective.

Lejeune's own account of his origins, written after arrival in the USSR, echoed this narrative. In 1931, International Red Aid, usually known by its Russian acronym MOPR, published a brochure, 'The Last of the Communards', in solidarity with Communist political prisoners. In this text, strewn with errors in the transcription of proper names, attributed to an author then aged eighty-four and without any previous literary publications, Lejeune evoked his childhood as follows:

I was born in 1847 in the village of Bagnolet. At this time, our hamlet was situated outside the fortifications of Paris. Today, Bagnolet is the prolongation of the working-class districts of Belleville and Ménilmontant. Our family had difficulty getting by. We were seven children. My father worked for a saddler in the neighbouring village. Every day, I took him his breakfast. I was seven at the time. I was afraid then of crossing the fields on my own. Anyway, it was not very easy: you had to make sure you did not spill the food or let it go cold on the way. My father did not play around and we got a good beating if we did not behave.

Lejeune went to school at the age of nine. However, the teacher did not pay much attention to him: 'I was from a poor family, whereas he was mainly interested in the children of rich peasants who brought him gifts.' Lejeune was not yet eleven when, deaf to his mother's protests, his father obliged him to leave school and get a job as a grocer's boy, with a shopkeeper who would oversee his apprenticeship for two years. However, life was not easy in the master's house. He was treated with brutality: he was badly fed, and made to sleep in a cubbyhole so tight it was impossible to turn around. Waking at dawn and working until late, he was driven to a drudgery he describes as 'beyond my strength', complaining that he was not allowed to sit down even once during a normal day.

But this labour was also an apprenticeship in autonomy and revolt. As time went on, Lejeune got to know boys older than himself and realised that 'you could find a marvellous job and not be pushed around'. As a result he switched employers several times, quick to leave anywhere he felt exploited or where the boss was a drunk. After moving from grocery to grocery, Lejeune was finally hired by a large herbalist's shop in central Paris, near to the recently completed *grands boulevards*. He gave up his apron for a jacket, as his boss requested, and prepared himself conscientiously for his new profession: 'I learned to choose medicinal herbs and compose medications. I had enough leisure time and I began to study, alone at first, then I signed up for courses in herbalism.'[2]

Lejeune undertook this apprenticeship in a city that had

grown enormously in the last twenty years: by 1851 Paris had one million inhabitants, two million in 1870. Its working-class population was by far the largest in France, estimated in 1866 as more than 450,000, employed in small and medium-sized workshops but also in the spreading factories. None of the proletariats in France rivalled the militancy of the Parisians. In the last two years of the Empire, strikes multiplied, and the Federal Chamber of Parisian Workers' Societies, an alliance of up to 30,000 people closely linked to the First International co-founded by Karl Marx, extended its influence in working-class areas. The Paris proletariat found allies in wage-earners of all sorts: artisans, shopkeepers and marginals.

These multiplying popular classes no longer lived alongside the rich. Population growth, the radical urban ren-ovations ordered by Baron Haussmann, prefect of the Seine Department, and a sharp rise in rents, led to the displacement of the working population from the city centre towards the periphery: Montmartre, La Villette and Belleville on the right bank, Bercy, Ivry and Grenelle on the left. Social antagonisms were inscribed in the very geography of the capital: the *beaux quartiers* of the centre and west seemed caught in a pincer by the proletarian north, south and east. It is therefore no surprise that this great subversive city had been denied all municipal rights by the emperor since his coup d'état in 1851.

At his workplace, Lejeune started to observe the different classes of customers who came in and out, from rich patrons to delivery boys. He began to develop an understanding of the inequities of the city, and a sensitivity to injustice. From this incipient interest in social issues came his first political act, to join the Society of Freethinkers.

These *libres-penseurs* had emerged as a significant force during the revolution of 1848, which overthrew the bourgeois monarchy of Louis-Philippe and proclaimed the Second Republic. They contested religious dogmatism (associated with the Catholic Church) and monarchy in the name of Reason and the Republic. After Louis-Napoleon Bonaparte's 1851 coup and his establishment of the authoritarian Second Empire, freethinkers had gone underground or into exile. But as the regime began to make concessions on freedom of speech and association in the 1860s, against a backdrop of economic crisis and growing political opposition, they re-emerged, organising secular funerals and mutual aid for non-believers. They also played a key role in the foundation of the First International and the organisation of anti-clerical congresses in Geneva and Naples. In 1866, Emile Eudes, future general of the Commune, founded the journal *La Libre Pensée*, which became a rallying-point for opponents of the regime. In his memoir, Lejeune explained the importance of the freethinkers for his political development:

> At the time there were no workers' unions. Nor was there a political party of the working class. That is why the Society of Freethinkers was considered an important revolutionary organisation. It is true that its activity was limited to the organisation and participation of its members in non-religious funerals, but it was a very rare thing at the time and, above all in the countryside, it was an act of opposition to the regime. It was at these non-religious funerals that I got to know future militants of the Commune, such as Eude[s], [Théophile] Ferret [Ferré] and others.

Non-religious funerals allowed republicans to gather in public. When police surveillance allowed, there would be speeches in praise of the deceased that rapidly took on a subversive hue, ending with cries of '*Vive la République!*' or, even more radically, '*Vive la République démocratique et sociale!*'[3]

The young Adrien was already involved in the politics of France; he belonged to an embryonic proletariat with an emerging consciousness, both socialist and republican, and was in contact with future actors of the Commune. But history was about to accelerate, and change his life utterly. In July 1870, the French emperor took the fateful decision to declare war on expansionist Prussia, ostensibly over the issue of the succession to the Spanish throne. On 4 September, in the midst of military humiliation – the emperor himself had been taken prisoner at Sedan – an immense crowd, bourgeois and non-bourgeois, descended on the Palais-Bourbon, seat of France's parliament: the Second Empire was overthrown, and the Third Republic proclaimed. However, the troops of the 'Iron Chancellor' Bismarck soon surrounded Paris and, during the severe winter of 1870–71, asphyxiated the capital.

In February 1871, France, predominantly rural and religious, tired of war and fearful of revolutionary upheaval, elected an Assembly dominated by a provincial conservative ready to make peace with Berlin. The Assembly chose as head of the executive Adolphe Thiers, an ambiguous figure who was both monarchist and liberal. Republican Paris, on the other hand, had clearly chosen the left and the continuation of war. This conflict between Paris and the provinces was rapidly aggravated when the new government decreed a pay cut for the National Guard and an end to the wartime moratorium on rent, thus drastically affecting the income of the lower classes at a time of severe economic dislocation. To add insult to injury, as part of the peace deal, the Prussian army was allowed by the French government to symbolically occupy Paris for two days.

On 18 March 1871, the Thiers government, now withdrawn from the restive capital to the safety of royalist Versailles, tried to disarm the National Guard in Paris. On the heights of Montmartre, the army's failed attempt to seize the Guard's cannon – which had been partly financed by popular subscription – triggered an uprising in the working-class arrondissements of the north. Crowds converged on the Hôtel de Ville and, that evening, only miles from the village of Bagnolet, the 'organised apocalypse' of the Paris Commune began: seventy-one days of passion and chaos which inspired and terrified.

2

Lejeune, Communard

How could one be a Communard among the prosperous fruit-growers of sleepy Bagnolet, who seemed the very antithesis of revolutionary Parisian workers? The poet Jean-Baptiste Clément, who knew Bagnolet well, was not kind to the village inhabitants: 'For a long time I have wanted to say what I think to these backward *croquants* [yokels] who grow fat under the church bells, in the land of redcurrants and sour wine'. The poet wrote this on the front page of *Le Cri du peuple*, one of the Commune's most important and radical newspapers, on 3 May 1871, during the critical period when the grip of the Versaillais was tightening on Paris. He went on:

> The poor man fights and dies. There are widows and orphans. The people are sublime, and they are insulted. I am irritated by the ignorance of these bumpkins; their cowardice exasperates me. In Bagnolet, there were nevertheless some brave citizens who wanted to proclaim the Commune, the revolutionary Commune. What did the *croquants* do? They went to the Prussians and told them that the tramps and great unwashed

were opposed to their property. They said that the reds and the envious were going to take away their wives and children, settle in their homes and kick them out onto the street.

Yesterday, four National Guards went outside the ramparts to the outskirts of Bagnolet, where in the past they often used to drink a litre of wine and eat some rabbit, which the local publicans did not complain about. What did the *croquants* do? They went to alert the gendarmes and, cowards that they are, handed them over.

Ah, Jacques Bonhomme [a peasant rebel of the Hundred Years' War], badly-dressed, nasty, ill-shaven, you have let yourself become more royalist than the king. Those whom you now call reds and resentful one day came out of their holes. They wanted the air and sun to be for everyone. They took pitchforks, sticks, pikes and old rifles and threw themselves at those who had reduced you to servitude. They died in order to enrich you, and yet their children have remained poor and you hate them, and you insult them.[1]

These *croquants* of Bagnolet forgot that they owed their rights to property, freedom and justice to those very 'reds' who had overthrown feudalism in 1789. Instead, they hated those Parisian *misérables* whose custom enriched them and who were demanding their own place in the sun. Clément signed off with menacing virulence:

You are the cries of the Imperial plebisciters, the shrimps of progress, the deserters from justice, the refusers of freedom. We owe to you the misfortunes we suffer, and you don't even have the prudence to blush! So long as your vines flourish, your wheat grows, your fat mugs get ruddier, your bellies get rounder, and your purses fill, you don't give a damn that freedom is being murdered and we are dying with it. For the time being, that is.

The *croquants* of Bagnolet were therefore not just recalcitrant but downright hostile to revolutionary Paris. However, local historian Jean-Pierre Gast points to a saving grace, the act of vengeance which Clément's outburst announces. On 2 May 1871, Roussel, a Communard police captain, went to Bagnolet accompanied by some Fédérés with the aim of arresting members of the municipality and several other people suspected of treason. Some things did happen in sleepy and smug Bagnolet.[2]

What's more, a local man, Adrien Lejeune, was in the thick of things in Paris. Jacques Duclos, in his centenary book, *The Paris Commune Storming the Heavens* (adopting Marx's famous phrase), wrote of the Bagnoletais's exploits: 'They were still fighting at a few barricades of the 20th arrondissement. Behind one of them was the last survivor of the Commune, Albert [*sic*] Lejeune, who died in the Soviet Union in 1942.'[3] At the centenary, the municipal bulletin of Bagnolet proudly declared of the local hero and veteran of the Commune: 'Gun in hand, he took part in that great epic of which Lenin could say: "it taught the European proletariat to pose in concrete terms the problems of social Revolution". Adrien Lejeune, the twenty-four-year-old sergeant in the National Guard who rallied to the Communards, took part in the struggle ... But on the morning of 28 May 1871, Mme Fochère, his own godmother, denounced him to the Versaillais.'

In *La Vie Ouvrière*, organ of Communist-controlled union the CGT, Jacqueline Jourdan gave a version of events that was a little less combative, but still positive: 'During that tragic week, Adrien Lejeune fought notably at the barricades raised in the rue de Ménilmontant and rue de Belleville. ... He spent the night in a fire station, then was arrested in the rue de Belleville.'[4] He had wanted to go to the 20th arrondissement, where the centre of resistance had moved. In any case, Jourdan concluded, this arrest spared him from being massacred like the last resistors.

Back in 1931, in the section of his autobiography entitled 'We Raise the Red Flag. On the Barricades', Lejeune painted for his Comintern readers the portrait of a tough, uncompromising Communard. He began by capturing the jingoistic frenzy in the summer of 1870, which only a few lucid revolutionaries like himself could resist. Some agents provocateurs, dressed in workers' overalls in order to mingle more easily with the popular masses, zealously prepared the ground for the declaration of war. They shouted 'To Berlin!' to which Lejeune and his comrades replied: 'Long live peace!' Emile Eudes, an ardent and convinced republican, tried to organise an uprising in Paris, but it failed. The rebels were dispersed or arrested. Naturally, Lejeune observed, Eudes would have been shot were it not for the revolution of 4 September 1870. The proclamation of the Republic saved his life.

Lejeune himself was not called up at the outbreak of the Franco–Prussian War, being exempted from military service on health grounds. However, during the conflict he volunteered for the National Guard, the increasingly radicalised citizens' militia which remained behind in Paris. This, he explained, was a strategic move. Other republicans did the same thing. They considered that, taking advantage of favourable circumstances, their presence in the military units could help overthrow the Empire and establish a republic. The Republic was eventually proclaimed, but it did not justify their hopes; for them, it was a 'Republic without republicans'. The monarchists remained in their positions of power and did nothing to further the success of the Republic. As for the defence against the advancing Prussians, this was not, Lejeune later claimed, sufficiently organised.

On 18 March 1871, when the National Guard stationed on the Butte de Montmartre refused to hand over its cannons to the elected government, Lejeune and his comrades joined the insurrection. They went into the barracks to get weapons, for not long before, they had been taken from them. No one stood in their way: that morning, the government had fled to Versailles and concentrated there the troops still loyal to them, leaving the barracks unguarded. But despite this initial success, in Lejeune's eyes, serious errors were subsequently made. He wrote in later accounts, espousing a familiar Marxist-Leninist analysis, that the Communards should have organised a real defence of the city, prevented the government from leaving Paris and seized the houses of the bourgeois who had joined Thiers. In short, they should have opposed a genuine workers' power to the Versaillais, who began to prepare the offensive against Paris. Instead, on 26 March, elections were organised for the Council of the Commune. As for Thiers, who had rebuffed attempts at mediation by moderate republican mayors in Paris, he wasted no time in concentrating the troops that Bismarck had put at his disposal since the armistice. By the time the Council elections were over, Thiers was ready to go on the offensive.

It was the working population of Paris that made the revolution and organised the Commune, even though there were still no sizeable factories offering mass employment, only small workshops. Many worked at home. There were no big stores, just small shops dispersed throughout the city. In its immense majority, Lejeune claimed in his later accounts, all this labouring population sympathised with and supported the Commune. However, he observed a disconnect between the cities and the countryside: 'Thiers and the clergy agitated in the provinces, especially in the countryside, with which we were not in contact.' For this reason, the inhabitants of the villages even close to Paris were hostile to the Parisians who came to the countryside on holidays: 'The peasants considered the city dwellers to be people who had come to spoil or steal the apples and cherries in their orchards.' Lejeune therefore 'wanted to teach [his] compatriots a lesson'. At 'the beginning of April [sic]', he entered Bagnolet, with other members of the National Guard, to the sound of a drum. They crossed the village and stopped in front of the *mairie*. The secretary of the *mairie*, Connac, a devoted monarchist, took to his heels. When the red flag replaced the tricolour, there was 'genuine panic'.

This incident as recounted by Lejeune confirmed the existence, just beyond the city walls, of 'rustic' hostility to the Commune. Further south, the strategically important village of Vitry – another future red bastion – was occupied by Fédérés. Coexistence was not easy between these armed Parisian workers and the local population, not least because the latter were obliged to feed the visitors and bolster their fortifications.[5] Certainly, there are records of pro-Communard manifestations in nearby settlements like Coulommiers, Souppes and Nemours, but on 13 May 1871, the Versaillais *Journal officiel de la République française* could, with some justification, present the Paris suburbs as victims of a year of terrible events. Ravaged a few months previously by the Prussian invasion, these areas were now suffering all the misfortunes of civil war. The impoverished inhabitants, scarcely delivered from foreign occupation, had seen their houses, possessions, and anything else spared by the enemy, destroyed by French artillery bombardment. Forced to flee to escape the necessity of becoming either victims or accomplices of the insurrection, they wandered without shelter, without bread, without clothes, begging for the pity of already exhausted villages. Whole families camped out in abandoned ruins, with nothing to eat but the bits of mouldy bread other indigents might share with them.[6] As for the provincial cities, Communes were organised in some of them, notably Marseille and Lyon, but these attempts failed, reinforcing the sense of a war between revolutionary Paris and reactionary 'rurals'. Nevertheless, back in Paris, the Communards still hoped to prevail and it seemed to Lejeune in retrospect that this would have happened if only their leaders had followed the words of Marat: 'To be human and just, it is better to spill a few drops of blood rather than make rivers of pure blood flow.'

According to his account, Lejeune served in the National Guard from the beginning to the bloody end of the Commune, and seemed unafraid to follow the ruthless precept of Marat if need be : 'I stood guard on the fortifications of Paris and in front of the city gates. We made round-ups and searched suspect houses at night. That's how it was during the Commune.' He also states that he was well-connected, claiming to have known, since before the insurrection, Théophile Ferré, chief of the revolutionary police, Alexis Trinquet, councillor for the militant 20th arrondissement, and Aimé Félix Pyat, a member of the Committee of Public Safety. But during the Commune, 'each of us was at his post. I was just a man in the rank and file, they were leaders and we did not have time to see each other.' Lejeune also knew the famed 'Red Virgin', Louise Michel, a redoubtable anarchist schoolteacher and poet: 'but what Communard did not know her? She was a woman extraordinarily committed to the cause of the Revolution. How many calumnies and insanities have been spread about this heroine?'

The Commune was 'above all war, civil war'. Nevertheless, Lejeune recognised that the Commune introduced some progressive measures during its brief lifetime, noting that the decree cancelling rent arrears was of 'great importance to the working population', along with the decrees on the separation of Church and State, and on public education. However, in a situation of civil war, the main concern of the National Guard was not to let the Versaillais enter Paris. Lejeune recalled the treacherous role of one Ducâtel, a city roadworks foreman, who, on 21 May, indicated to the Versaillais that some of the western bastions of the Paris fortifications were unprotected. Regular troops, under the command of General MacMahon, surrounded the city and went on the attack, quickly seizing the *beaux quartiers* of the south-west and obliging the defenders of the Commune to fall back towards the centre. Barricades had been erected in secure places before the troops invaded.

As soon as Lejeune and his comrades heard the news of the Versaillais entering Paris, they threw themselves on the barricades and the final struggle began. In retrospect, Lejeune paid homage to the romantic heroism of the Communards while acknowledging their military shortcomings:

> Was there a defence plan? Probably there was. There was also a certain organisation of the defence, because we were supplied with munitions and even food. We were relieved. We went to rest, slept, then returned to our posts. However, we acted rather as revolutionaries who had long been ready for sacrifice, who had decided to die and not surrender, rather than as military men serving under the command of leaders.

The Communards defended the barricades in districts across Paris, but by the evening of 24 May, the invading troops had taken the Hôtel de Ville. Within another three days of fighting, the last pockets of resistance were in the north, where the Parisian insurrection had begun. Seeing the hopelessness of their situation, they knew that the cause of the Commune was lost, but, as Lejeune recalls, 'we fought on, falling back from barricade to barricade, extracting a heavy price for our lives.'

It was thus that Adrien Lejeune claimed to have ended up on the barricades of the rue des Pyrénées, in Belleville, in the night of the 27 to 28 May:

> [Gabriel] Ranvier [mayor of the 20th arrondissement] and Trinquet came to see us and led me to a small bar nearby, so I could rest and regain my strength, since I had not eaten for at least twenty-four hours. Ranvier told me that he was going to

try and get out of Paris, because the cause was lost. I wanted to go with him, but it was easier to go it alone and we went our separate ways. In the morning, I was made prisoner on a barricade.

Lejeune was therefore involved in the last days of fighting by the Communards, who were methodically crushed by an army far superior in numbers, equipment and training. Despite undoubted acts of heroism and even military skill, this disputatious and amateurish citizens' militia was doomed to fail. Lenin's Bolsheviks would not hesitate to draw lessons from that defeat, noting the lack of organisation and insufficient harshness of the Communards, despite the hostage-taking, round-ups and searches that Lejeune claims to have taken part in.

What happened to Lejeune after his arrest? For Bagnolet's municipal bulletin, 'the threat of being shot hung over Adrien Lejeune. He was saved thanks to the eloquent plea of his lawyer.' According to Jacqueline Jourdan, 'he was incarcerated in the military prison of Noailles and tried on 12 February 1872, by the 19th Permanent Conseil de Guerre [military tribunal] of the first military division, in Versailles.' Lejeune's own account was typically dramatic:

An officer approached, emptied his sack of insults and, after calling us a bunch of good-for-nothings, ordered us to follow him to the place reserved for prisoners. Hours passed and we learned that, apparently on the orders of Versailles, we were no longer to be shot. We were ordered to turn our coats inside out, as well as our hats and thus attired, chained in twos, we were taken to Versailles.

The humiliated prisoners had to face the ferocity of a bourgeois crowd hell-bent on revenge after ten weeks of the 'riff-raff' in power. Lejeune remembered a priest who passed them and began to yell: 'Shoot them all! God will know how to tell between those who are guilty and those who are right.' The crowd, growing heated, tried to gouge the Communards' eyes out with the points of their umbrellas. The captives were marched down the rue Lafayette, in the *beaux quartiers*, before crossing the Bois de Boulogne where they were told to stop. Eventually General Galliffet, who played a notorious role in the repression of the Commune, approached them, and Lejeune describes how he made them line up so he could see every one, and began to take his pick:

'You must have taken part in the revolution of '48. Step out!'
'You look more intelligent, step out!'
'You, the wounded fellow, step out!'

The selected prisoners' mothers and wives begged Galliffet for mercy, but he simply told them: 'Your tears do not touch me. I'm not one of them.' He called out twenty-five men. Lejeune was not among them. An officer of the gendarmes, who had been busy tracking down Communards, marched up to Galliffet and, saluting, said: 'Your Excellency, I request the honour of commanding the firing squad.' Some prisoners were made to dig the trench in the presence of the condemned, who were then shot. The escort of infantrymen was replaced by horsemen who herded the remainder along the road to Versailles. It was only a matter of luck, then, that Lejeune did not join his comrades in a mass grave.

Lejeune eventually found himself in a floating prison at 'Port-Oré' [Port d'Auray], off the Breton coast, where he awaited trial: 'We were dying of hunger, for we had not eaten anything since the day we were given bread in Versailles.' However, he was surprised and cheered to meet up with other surviving comrades. The food was appalling, but relatives and friends were authorised to bring provisions, 'that way we could share with those who had nothing.' This group solidarity encouraged revolutionary audacity in defiance of the prison regime. An officer arrived, accompanied by several sailors, and began to question them about their names, ages and religions. Lejeune was the first of his group to be questioned, and when asked about his religion, told the truth:

> I replied that I belonged to no confession.
> 'But you did do your First Communion?'
> 'No,' I replied.
> 'But you were baptised?'
> 'I don't know. I don't remember it'.

The other comrades followed this freethinker's example: 'The officer was furious, and if there had only been a few of us we would have been put in irons and kept like that until we had remembered our religion. But there were a lot of us, and we did not suffer for our audacity'.

After four or five months in these conditions, the prisoners were informed that the minister Jules Simon was to visit their ship. Naturally, they planned a disturbance for the occasion. However, they did not have this pleasure, for having been badly received by other prisoners, the minister did not dare continue his visit. In his seventh month of detention, Lejeune learned that a group of policemen had arrived in the prison and were beginning to interrogate each prisoner. They were summoned one by one to a big cabin where some individuals were seated at a table heaped with papers. Lejeune's turn came. He tells how he entered the room 'fearlessly':

'Are you the son Lejeune?'

'Indeed I am,' I replied.

'You're not as sure of yourself today as you were when you raised the red flag over Bagnolet.'

'You are mistaken and are attributing to me a power I did not have.'

'Yes, I know. It's not you who did it, but it was on your instigation that this took place. You are well known to the people who accuse you.'

'And who are these people?'

'Madame Fomer [*sic*], woman of independent means; Poinquier, gravedigger; Gril [*sic*] policeman, Conak [*sic*] secretary to the *mairie*, and Ledier [*sic*], wine merchant. Do you know them?'

To flush out the informers, Lejeune replied facetiously: 'But of course I know them. They are my benefactors. I know I can always count on them. They know I'm a good worker, and besides they are my friends.' The policemen 'could no longer tell if I was making fun of them or if they were mistaken'.

A month later, Lejeune found himself in front of a Conseil de Guerre, one of the twenty-four military tribunals set up to judge the Communards in what is considered to be the harshest wave of state repression in France's history. He was threatened with Article 5, which meant the death penalty. But he harboured a few hopes, because his mother had known the mayor of Bagnolet, Adolphe Viénot, since childhood, and went to ask him to certify that Lejeune was with his family during the Commune. 'Of course, it will be my pleasure to do this for you,' replied the mayor. 'Come and see me at the town hall and I will give you this certificate.' His mother went to the *mairie* and took the paper with effusive thanks, rushed back to the house and read: 'I, the undersigned, Vieillot [*sic*], mayor of Bagnolet, certify that the young Adrien Lejeune lived with his parents in Bagnolet. But since 18 March 1871 his place of residence has been unknown.' Lejeune's father was not at all surprised by this treachery, but his mother was furious to have been made a fool of in this way.

At the end of January 1872, Lejeune was handcuffed by the gendarmes, put on a boat, and then transported to Versailles in a prison wagon. When he finally appeared before the tribunal, Lejeune claims indeed to have been saved by an 'ingenious defence lawyer'. Thanks to friends, his father managed to line up a well-known lawyer whose name Lejeune could not recall. However, before the trial, this illustrious defence lawyer had not yet shown up, and he was worried. After five or ten minutes he found himself in front of the military judges, and his lawyer had still not arrived. Exactly five minutes before the hearing began, a young man ran up to him:

'Are you Lejeune?'
  'Yes, that's me.'
  'Your lawyer cannot come, I'm the one who will defend you.'

'But how can this happen, we haven't even spoken to each other?'

'That doesn't matter. I just ask of you one thing: don't say a word, act as if you're mute.'

The hearing began and the charge sheet was read out: wearing a uniform, handling illegal weapons, using these weapons, etc. Lejeune was accused of being 'a freethinker, unbalanced, a socialist, an enemy of property, etc, etc …' Then, Lejeune writes in his autobiography, his young defence lawyer stood up. 'He praised me. He said I was a model son, an excellent worker and, suddenly, he cried out, making a dramatic gesture to the court: "But how can this young man be an enemy of property, when he is himself a property-owner?"' After this assertion, as unexpected for Lejeune as it was for the judges, his conviction and sentence were pronounced: five years' imprisonment. Lejeune estimated that 'the affair lasted twenty minutes in total.' He continued, 'You should have seen the faces of the witnesses for the prosecution when the defence lawyer declared I was a property-owner …' So the Last Communard claimed to have been saved from the firing squad because he was alleged at his hearing to be a man of property.

How trustworthy is Lejeune's account of the last days of the Commune and its aftermath? It certainly chimes with the two most famous accounts by former Communards, Maxime Vuillaume's *Mes cahiers rouges* and Prosper-Olivier Lissagaray's still authoritative, if unashamedly partisan, *History of the Paris Commune of 1871*: the doomed last stands on the slopes of Belleville, the denunciations, the Jardin du Luxembourg and other picturesque parks transformed into abattoirs, the public humiliation of prisoners by inhabitants of the *beaux quartiers*, the summary executions ordered by Galliffet, incarceration in floating prisons and fortresses on the Breton coast. However, in order to gain a more precise and accurate picture of Lejeune's involvement in those events, it is interesting to check his stories against the archives of the authorities who arrested and judged Lejeune and the other Communards. The account he put his name to in 1931 seems to have been embellished, to say the least.

According to the documents kept in the military archives, Lejeune had already appeared before the 3rd Conseil de Guerre on 24 August 1871.[7] It is recorded that a short exchange followed:

'Were you a member of the National Guard?'

'I was in the 28th Battalion during the siege. I was a sergeant. The people of Bagnolet then went home and were not members of the National Guard. This battalion was in fact dissolved and I did not go when I was called back during the Commune.'

'How come you were arrested in Paris?'

'I often went to Paris on business and in the month of May, around the 22nd I could not leave, the National Guards arrested me and took me to the prison of La Roquette which I left on the evening of the 27th when the guards opened the gates. I was given a rifle and stationed at a barricade in the rue Ménilmontant. I did not fire, I put down my rifle, and I ran away to Belleville.'

'Where were you arrested?'

'The morning of Sunday 28th in the rue de Paris in Belleville where I had taken refuge.'

Rather than the 'revolutionary audacity' he claims to have displayed during his time in the floating prison, Lejeune is on record protesting that he was coerced into taking part in the insurrection, denying his voluntary involvement in order to avoid punishment. According to the statement of the police detective, Lejeune had indeed been a delegate for the 20th arrondissement, and had played an active role in the Commune. The statement of the accused, it was concluded, 'who seemed rather uneasy in his replies, is completely mendacious'.

Lejeune was taken out of the military prison in Noailles to appear, on 21 January 1872, before the 19th Conseil de Guerre, accused of 'participation in the Parisian insurrection'. He answered again that he had 'never' been a member of the National Guard during the Commune. Instead, he had stayed at home in Bagnolet 'without being bothered'. After the armistice of February 1871, he had returned his rifle to the battalion's barracks, despite the fact that no battalion had been disarmed. As for the punitive raid on the *mairie* of Bagnolet, Lejeune admitted he knew of a police officer in Paris by the name of Roussel, but he did not know of what arrondissement, and had 'never had the slightest relation' with him. Concerning the allegation that he had carried out administrative responsibilities at the *mairie* of the 20th arrondissement, Lejeune claimed to have gone there three or four times to obtain a pass to leave Paris, but was not appointed as a delegate for issuing passes and organising food supplies.

However, under persistent questioning, Lejeune admitted to having witnessed Roussel's raid on Bagnolet. He had seen the local policeman Grille arrested in retaliation for the arrest of some National Guards a fortnight before, but he was just one of a crowd of sixty people. He also heard two revolver shots aimed at the *mairie*'s secretary, Connac, but could not identify the fleeing would-be assassin. Lejeune was then questioned on his beliefs prior to the Commune, which was often a way in which the military courts tried to ascertain the accused's guilt. Here, too, the accused was evasive: he admitted to attending in the course of February 1870 the non-religious funeral of a certain Antoine, a freethinker, whose ideas he shared. But his 'speech' at Antoine's graveside was from a piece of paper which a relative or friend had requested him to read out.

Finally, Lejeune was asked about how he came to be arrested in Paris at the end of the Bloody Week. While he was trying to leave through the Porte de Vincennes, on Monday 22 May, he encountered some National Guards who did not let him pass and arrested him. The following day, he was taken to a police station and told to join the Guard. When he refused he was taken to the prison of La Roquette, which was already brimming with enemies of the Commune, some of whom, including the archbishop of Paris, would be executed during those final days. 'Fearing things would take a turn for the worse', Lejeune finally donned the uniform of the National Guard 'as the price of my freedom'. He was given a rifle and led to the barricade of the rue Ménilmontant. Lejeune claimed that they had not even given him packets of cartridges for his rifle. He stayed at the barricade for 'an hour or two at most; from there I left for Belleville after leaving my rifle behind the barricade. I spent the night of 27 to 28 in a fire station in Belleville.'

One last exchange tried to ascertain his membership of the rebel militia:

'Were you ever a member of the 174th battalion?'

'No.'

'Do you know about the formation of the "Children of Père Duchêne" battalion, and were you an artilleryman during the Commune?'

'I don't know what you're talking about.'

Lejeune therefore denied not only his voluntary participation in the most radical battalion created by the virulent, foul-mouthed newspaper *Le Père Duchêne* (a revival of the journal published in 1790–94), but any voluntary participation in the Parisian insurrection. If Lejeune had a rifle, he claimed to not have had any ammunition. He described himself as simply a witness to the raid led by Roussel and his Communard comrades on the *mairie* of Bagnolet. He claimed that his incendiary graveside speeches were delivered at the request of others.

In the rest of the trial, which appears to have lasted much longer than the 'twenty minutes' claimed by Lejeune in his autobiography, the statements of several witnesses were considered. The first witness was Marguerite Boudin, 'widow Faucheur', the 'Godmother Fochère' who had allegedly 'denounced' our Communard. She declared:

I do not know this young man and I cannot give any information on him. I only know his father. He lives in Bagnolet, where he is a fruit-merchant. I cannot tell you if he took part in the insurrection. All I can say is that, five or six days before the end of the insurrection, I met him on the boulevard Puebla, opposite the Ménilmontant market. He was smartly dressed and was watching, with other passers-by, some artillerymen of the Fédérés. As soon as he saw me, he slipped away. His presence in this place did surprise me, given that he lives in Bagnolet.

If we are to believe this succinct and slightly obscure statement, the widow Faucheur was neither godmother nor exactly a police informer, and Lejeune's direct participation in the Commune's doomed military struggle is only suggested by some shifty behaviour.

More compromising, however, was the statement by Mathieu Poinquier, a gravedigger from Bagnolet, who asserted at the outset that he was 'neither a servant nor a relative nor an ally of the accused Lejeune'. He declared to the court:

> I have known Lejeune since his childhood; he professes fanatical opinions. He did not miss the procession and funeral of no less than *six* freethinkers buried in the cemetery of Bagnolet. At each of these funerals he made speeches which occasionally offended those in attendance. In his farewells to the deceased and after having expressed the most crude and offensive insults to priests, the government and property-owners, he would shout: 'Farewell, brother, we stay here, for the good cause.' After one of these antisocial ceremonies, I saw him slapped, outside the cemetery, in front of the gate to this holy place, by people outraged by his speech. He did not have the courage to fight back.

According to Poinquier, during the Commune, Lejeune, wearing a *chapeau à la Caussidière* (a hat worn by Communards in homage to Marc Caussidière, the 'red' prefect of Paris

36

police during the revolution of 1848), with a peacock feather in it and a red belt around his waist, 'went in and out of Paris as he pleased, on a simple signal he gave to the Fédérés'. Poinquier concluded: 'I think he was behind the incidents at Bagnolet on 2 May 1871, the day a hundred *enragés* invaded the locality. This is all I know about this young man, who in my view simply adopted a long time ago the advanced ideas of his father.'

So Lejeune seems to have already made a sulphurous reputation for himself among the *croquants* of his home village. It was then the turn of Adénisse Connac, the secretary to the *mairie* of Bagnolet, to try and nail the Communard. He had learned that Lejeune was indeed a delegate at the *mairie* of Belleville with responsibility for food supplies. He maintained 'close relations' with monsieur Roussel, the police captain for Belleville during the Commune, and it was this same Roussel who arrived one day in Bagnolet with a list of fourteen people including the mayor, his deputy, several municipal councillors and other people that 'we knew were hostile to Lejeune among others'.

On the day of the raid, Roussel arrived in a removal carriage with twenty-five men disguised as workers. Roussel knew very well that all the people he planned to arrest were just then at the *mairie*. Lejeune had come to Bagnolet the day before. At a given moment, these twenty-five men irrupted into the *mairie*. They locked the men in their offices; Roussel drew out his list and pointed first at police officer Grille, who was promptly taken away. Then it was Connac's turn. Fortunately for the secretary, 'I was able to escape them. Roussel fired two revolver shots at me.' That said, Connac could not assure the prosecutor that he had actually seen Lejeune in this group, although he claimed that it was his younger brother who held the bridle of the horse harnessed to the carriage into which they had thrown M. Grille. But Connac reiterated that 'it is common knowledge that Lejeune was the most fanatical man in the area.' Asked if Lejeune was feared in Bagnolet, he replied categorically: 'He was much feared.'

Connac's testimony was followed by that of Julien Grille, the rural policeman arrested by Roussel in Bagnolet. He too remembered the young Lejeune's outbursts before the fall of the Second Empire: when monsieur Antoine's body was lowered into the ground, Lejeune had said 'there was no more need for priests, that the government was unacceptable, and that there was no God'. What's more, he had heard from many people that Lejeune had a job at the *mairie* of Belleville and that he was close to police officers there 'which he would use one day against the inhabitants of Bagnolet'. The accused was 'an intrepid republican', who 'inspired terror' in his home village.

Lejeune's denial of his involvement seemed to be corroborated by the statement of Ledieu, a wine merchant, which also contradicted the claims made by Connac. But, according to the judges, it was 'easy to see in Ledieu a devoted friend of the accused, influenced by the same ideas, while we can see in monsieur Connac a very pronounced antipathy based no doubt upon the bad information that public opinion spread about the accused'. On 6 February 1872, the judges of the Conseil de Guerre drew up the following report on Lejeune:

After the insurrectional movement of 18 March, Lejeune, Adrien Félix, unmarried, made only a few brief appearances in Bagnolet. Every day he went to Paris and he only returned to his family in the evening. While recognising that the accused may have had to go to Paris from time to time on business, it is difficult to believe that these absences had to be repeated every day and last into the night. According to the declarations of witnesses and information gathered by the police, it is public knowledge that Lejeune had a job at the 20th arrondissement during the Commune. These responsibilities, whatever they were, are sufficient to explain the long and frequent sojourns that the accused made in Paris.

However, despite the contradictory and patchy evidence, his well-known subversive opinions did suggest that there was no smoke without fire, and the report continued:

Barely aged twenty-three this young man displayed the ideas of a freethinker, and on attending civil funerals, he even dared to speak and made speeches so extravagant that they exasperated all those in attendance. When one sees this young man have the audacity to draw attention to himself in this way, it is no surprise to see him occupying during the Commune a post which would equally put him in public view.

There remained the fact that towards the end of May, 'at the moment when the insurrection called on the support of all its members to put up one last resistance to the regular troops entering Paris', Adrien Lejeune tried to flee. The judges mused:

Without being able to discover the motive for this decision, we note, however, that the accused let himself be slapped in the face at the gates to Bagnolet cemetery without fighting back; it could very well be the case that at a given moment he felt he did not have the courage to sacrifice his life for the Commune. Arrested by the Fédérés at the Porte de Vincennes, he was then taken to the prison of La Roquette. No doubt realising that his life was no safer in this place than among the rebels, he asked to wear the uniform of the National Guard and go and fight in the ranks of the insurrection.

Given that the investigators had found no less than four Lejeunes in the various battalions of the National Guard, it was finally impossible to ascertain if the accused had belonged to any of them. The court also concluded that the information gathered by the police detective on Lejeune's conduct and morality was 'very bad'. Consequently, it was decided that Lejeune should be condemned for carrying out unauthorised administrative responsibilities, wearing a uniform and carrying illegal weapons. A week later, the 19th Conseil de Guerre sentenced him to five years' imprisonment. He was also obliged to reimburse the costs of his trial.

The five years' detention would be a figure inflated by the authors of Lejeune's legend. In 1971, the people of Bagnolet were informed by its municipal bulletin that he served five years in an offshore prison and was then sent to a labour camp in New Caledonia, before being incarcerated in a fortress for having taken part in an escape plan. In *La Vie Ouvrière*, Jacqueline Jourdan demonstrated knowledge of at least part of Lejeune's dossier, reporting the sentence and the reasons for it correctly. But she added: 'After a second request for a pardon, his sentence was reduced to four years in detention. Then he was deported to New Caledonia, from which he did not return until after the amnesty, in 1880.' Obviously, in the Communist imagination, the Last Communard, a precious relic of their implacable struggle against the ruling class, could not be freed before the final amnesty: he had to embody the full calvary of these revolutionary martyrs.

Lejeune's own version diverges from the ones cited above. The concluding passages of his autobiography are embellished and heroic, but devoid of tropical exoticism: instead, he says, he was sent back to Port d'Auray and, a few days later, put on a boat to the fortress of Port-Louis. Lejeune reports that the head of the fortress was 'a ferocious man, to such an extent that it would not have taken much more provocation for us to seize him and throw him down the well in the prison yard'. Lejeune and the other Communards were put among the common-law prisoners, including unsavoury elements who, Lejeune claims, were hell-bent on making the Communards' lives a misery: 'One of them had it in for me, and one day when I was standing near the wall of the cell, he ran up and head-butted my stomach. I had time to sidestep and his head crashed against the wall.'

Their spirit of resistance did not falter. Lejeune reports that one day, as a defiant revolutionary gesture, someone attached a little red pennant to the wall of their cell. The guard came and asked: 'What's that?' 'It's to scare away the flies,' someone replied. There weren't any flies. A few minutes later, Lejeune, presumably as the perceived ringleader, was summoned to see the director, with whom he claims he had already had several dealings. Lejeune refused to tell him who was behind the red pennant, and was thrown into a dungeon for his pains.

A year passed before three prisoners managed to escape from a neighbouring cell: they had been digging a hole at night for months. They took turns to do the work, and so that the bed never seemed unoccupied, they put a mannequin in it. The escapees were never recaptured. A few days later, Lejeune and his remaining comrades were transported to another Breton fortress, that of Belle-Île, where the regime was harsher than at Port-Louis: 'We were warned not to fight back, for they would have us; my comrades and I were not discouraged.' At mealtimes, these freethinking prisoners refused to say grace. Once more Lejeune was taken away to the dungeons, where he was soon joined by five other recalcitrants. In fact, 'our example was contagious and the other prisoners put up the same resistance. Eventually they left us in peace. We found four people who took turns to read out a prayer as the director demanded. But extra surveillance was arranged for us six.'

It was at this time that there began to be talk of a special pardons commission sitting in Paris. His father wrote to him that if he submitted a request for a pardon, he would surely be freed, because he had contacts with the minister of the interior. Lejeune replied that however much he wanted to recover his freedom, he would not ask his torturers for forgiveness. In the meantime, the Communards, who demanded their status be recognised as political prisoners, again attracted the wrath of the prison governor for refusing to have their heads shaved like common criminals. As a protest, they made lots of noise, sang, then climbed up onto the window ledge. The authorities threatened them, to no avail. However, after three days without food on a damp floor they were obliged to surrender. Lejeune himself was taken to the infirmary after an attack of rheumatism. When ten days later he rejoined his comrades, all had been shaven, like him. They were called 'Communard pigs', but did not miss an opportunity to annoy their guards.

Time passed. Lejeune's father wrote to him that the duration of his sentence had been reduced by a year; he had even calculated the day on which his son was to be freed. Lejeune found it hard to believe he would be released before the end of his original sentence. But he waited patiently. A month remained, two weeks, a week and finally a day; however, he was told nothing about an imminent release. After another week, he went to see the governor of the fortress, who stated curtly that without an order there was nothing he could do. In fact, he says, the order for his early release never came: 'It seems that that was the hardest period for me. They had dangled hope in front of me, in vain – there remained 365 days to serve. But everything comes to an end.' According to the last pages of Lejeune's account, there was another prison breakout, but he was not involved this time, and nor did he help the escapees. Nor, more importantly, is there any mention of doing time in New Caledonia. This absence is corroborated by the journals of the deported and studies on them. Lejeune was simply imprisoned in a fortress off the Breton coast.

What is also striking is that he denies ever benefitting from a one-year reduction in his sentence. Indeed, Lejeune's plea for a pardon further reinforces the complexity of this character and the construction of his myth.[8] On 9 December 1872, a request for a pardon, made by Lejeune's mother and sister and supported by Marc Dufraisse, a republican deputy in the National

Assembly, was rejected. The report to the pardons commission was negative, reiterating the charges against him and reminding them of his 'irreligious and antisocial' opinions: 'He does not have a criminal record, but information on his behaviour and morality are very unfavourable. ... There is no reason to propose a measure of clemency.' However, on 6 June 1874, his sentence was reduced to four years. Contrary to the allegation in his autobiography, Lejeune was indeed freed after that time, but in repressive conditions which pushed him to write in person to the minister of the interior on 30 October 1876:

> Sentenced to five years' imprisonment after the communalist insurrection, I had had the good fortune of seeing my punishment reduced to four years. Now free, having been able to settle definitively in Bagnolet (Seine) and wishing to get married, an obstacle, police surveillance, is thwarting my plans for the future. I therefore ask you, Monsieur le Ministre, to be so good as to spare me this punishment, which is an obstacle to my future happiness.

The director of general security informed the minister of the interior:

> During the Commune, Lejeune was a delegate to the *mairie* of the 20th arrondissement, and became known for his political fanaticism. However, I thought I could authorise him to return to the Department of the Seine, where today he lives with his parents in Bagnolet, but the information I have since received on him being generally unfavourable, I see no reason for further indulgence.

These requests for pardon and clemency were made in a climate that was extremely unfavourable to the Communards in general. Until 1876, the Third Republic was very much one 'without republicans': the rural-dominated Assembly would not hear of granting the amnesty requested each year by radical republicans, including Marc Dufraisse. The Senate would not have a republican majority until 1879. There followed a partial amnesty in that year, then a total one in 1880, the year of the first commemoration at the Mur des Fédérés and the election of Alexis Trinquet as municipal councillor for the district of Père-Lachaise. But Adrien Lejeune had at least been able to avoid the worst of the repression: he did not suffer execution or deportation.

Lejeune was both typical and atypical as a Communard. He shared some features of the 'men of 1871': like two-thirds of the rebels, he was in the prime of life; like half the Communards, he was unmarried; and, as in the immense majority of cases, he was a wage-earner. But his job as a pharmacist, and his belonging to a village on the outskirts of Paris, distinguished him from the journeymen and metal and construction workers of provincial origin who made up the majority of the rebel army. What's more, unlike many other Communards, Lejeune was literate and did not have a criminal past.

One thing we can be certain of: Adrien Félix Lejeune did take part in the Paris Commune. As a freethinker he belonged, from quite an early date, to the republican culture expressed by it. His extravagant costumes and 'fanatical' opinions were all part of the *'fête'* of March–May 1871. After his release, it is clear that he continued to hold subversive views. But it is also clear that the reality of Communard Lejeune lends itself with difficulty to the typical Communist hagiography. First of all, when cross-examined, Lejeune denied any participation in the Commune, unlike his comrade Louise Michel, who courageously declared to the 6th Conseil de Guerre: 'I don't want to defend myself, I don't want to be defended; I belong entirely to the social revolution and I declare I accept responsibility for all my acts. I accept it entirely and without restrictions.'[9] The accused was proud that she had offered to assassinate Thiers and burn down Paris. Despite such violence, she was not executed, and instead was deported to New Caledonia.

The Versaillais were certainly going to show greater clemency towards a woman, and Lejeune, like so many other Communards who had witnessed the carnage of the Bloody Week, was no doubt ready to say anything to save his skin. Indeed, Jacques Rougerie, in his pioneering work on the trials of the Communards, remarks that next to Louise Michel, the men of the Commune were a sorry bunch:

> These contradictory trials almost all turned into a rout. It was about who could dodge their responsibilities, when they were not tempted to pass them on to their neighbour. ... We see, if not a lack of moral courage, at least an extraordinary lack of substance. Or the incompetence of many of these men who thought they could become a revolutionary government ... Is that not one of the fundamental reasons for the failure of the Commune?[10]

That said, Alexis Trinquet, to whom Lejeune claimed to be close, had also declared to the 3rd Conseil de Guerre:

I was elected to the Commune by my fellow citizens; I paid with my person, I was on the barricades and I regret I was not killed there. Today, I will not put up with the sad spectacle of colleagues who, after having taken part in the action, refuse their share of responsibility. I am a rebel, and I don't deny it.[11]

He was given a life sentence of forced labour. Théophile Ferré, who as head of the revolutionary police had authorised the execution of six hostages at the prison of La Roquette, including the archbishop of Paris, on 25 May, declared before his judges: 'A member of the Paris Commune, I am in the hands of those who defeated it; if they want my head, let them take it! Never will I save my life through cowardice. Free I have lived, and free I will die! I entrust to the future my memory and my vengeance.'[12] He was executed by firing squad.

Adrien Lejeune does not seem to have fought completely voluntarily. After being found guilty, he pleaded for mercy from the state that ordered the Bloody Week, and did not embark on the 'red calvary' of deportees to Polynesia. But he was arrested in Paris during the last days of the Commune, and testimonies at his trial strongly suggest that he played a minor role in the insurrection. The records of Lejeune's revolutionary acts are as mixed as the rest of his life, combining idealism, myth-making and all-too-human frailty. Despite his very modest contribution, the legacy of the Paris Commune would dictate his next seventy years.

3

After the Commune

Information about Adrien Lejeune's life and activity after the Commune is sparse. However, accounts agree on his joining the French Communist Party soon after its foundation at the Congress of Tours in 1920. At the time of the centenary of the Commune, Duchet wrote in *France-URSS*: 'In 1922, he joined the French Communist Party. The main reason for his joining was the battle waged by the French Communists in defence of the Republic of the Soviets, in which Adrien recognised the direct descendant of the Paris Commune. His eyes were fixed on the east, on that country over which flies the flag of the Commune triumphant.'[1]

But the man who would become – thanks to sheer longevity – the very last of the Communards, did not make an impact on political life after the Commune. Despite his assertions of friendship, there is no trace of Lejeune in the books, journals and correspondence of the main actors of the insurrection. His name does not figure in the works by Vuillaume and Lissagaray. There is no mention of him in the sensationalist 1885 investigation into what had become of 'the men of modern Terror'.[2]

Lejeune's fate differed from that of his supposed fellow combatants. He did not return to the political scene, like Trinquet or Vaillant. He did not become a prominent Blanquist, like the Communard general Eudes, or that indefatigable anarchist campaigner Louise Michel. Nor did Lejeune have the symbolic importance of Zéphirin Camélinat, the founder of the First International and director of the mint under the Commune, who would also join the PCF, become its candidate for the presidency of the Republic in 1924, and whose death in March 1932 was the occasion for a huge Communist demonstration in the streets of Paris.

But Lejeune did not sink into bitterness, like Aimé Félix Pyat who, exiled to London, declared his disgust for mankind, presented himself as a martyr and considered his fellow refugees to be looters, thieves and cowards. Nor did Lejeune share the fiendish itinerary of the former police captain for the district of Père-Lachaise, Armand Roussel, nicknamed 'the Man with the Bombs'. Sentenced *in absentia* to twenty years' hard labour by the 3rd Conseil de Guerre, Roussel went on the run, first to Belgium, then to London where he attracted attention with 'the fanaticism of his socialist doctrines and the violence of his language at meetings of refugees'.[3] It seems that in October 1879, Roussel addressed from London, along with a group of other exiled Communards, his encouragement to the socialist workers' congress in Marseille, before disappearing from History.

Lejeune's life therefore seems to have been much less eventful and colourful than we are led to believe. But what would be useful for the PCF was the fact that he gravitated towards the Marxist current in French socialism rather than its reformist and anarcho-syndicalist rivals. This current, formerly divided between Edouard Vaillant, Jules Guesde, and Marx's own son-in-law Paul Lafargue, among others, finally united in 1905 in the SFIO, the French section of the Second International. In 1920, the SFIO split over the issue of Lenin's Third International. By joining the French section of this new International, Adrien Lejeune would follow the logic of the Bolshevik interpretation of the Commune: he had chosen the true heirs to the events of 1871.

In Paris, the amnesty of the Communards opened the way to the transformation of the Mur des Fédérés into what Pierre Nora dubbed a 'realm of memory'. Up until 1880 it was a shallow mass grave, which had fascinated and appalled visitors to that corner of Père-Lachaise: it was not uncommon to see a Parisian urchin kicking a Communard skull around as a football.[4] But in May of that year, socialist newspapers called for the first time for a gathering in front of the Mur. Subsequently, as Danielle Tartakowsky explains:

> The 'anniversaries of the Bloody Week' became a tradition that no one could fail to respect. Their effect was to shift the centre of gravity of the commemoration of the Paris Commune to the month of May, to the moment of its defeat and inflicted death, when elsewhere and previously it was celebrated in March. Honoured on the site of the final combat, the Commune was thus transcended.[5]

From 1882 onwards, graveside speeches were authorised, and flags were tolerated in the cemetery the following year. The placing of wreaths against the wall was another sign of the progressive appropriation of this sacred space. That said, the authorities were still wary of this return of the repressed: in February 1885, at the funeral of Jules Vallès, founder of *Le Cri du peuple*, the police intervened violently. Indeed, there was a fragile frontier between these gatherings in cemeteries and demonstrations on the public highway, which remained prohibited. However, in 1908, the victory of the left in the municipal elections enabled the unveiling of a marble plaque at the Mur des Fédérés. In 1910, no less than 30,000 people would demonstrate in front of it.

The battle over the meaning of the Paris Commune and the lessons to be drawn from its defeat were immediately engaged by Karl Marx. In *The Civil War in France*, Marx claimed to decipher the Commune, 'that sphinx so tantalising to the bourgeois mind'.[6] Faced with 'that monstrous gnome' Adolphe Thiers, the consummate intellectual expression of the French bourgeoisie's class-corruption, ready to conspire with a foreign enemy, Paris was the one great obstacle standing in the way of reaction. The Commune broke the spiritual force of repression, the 'parson-power'.[7] What's more, the Commune was the positive form of the 'social republic' ushered in but betrayed in 1848, while, in contrast with the 'cosmopolitan blacklegism' that characterised the Second Empire, the Commune 'admitted all foreigners to the honour of dying for an immortal cause'.[8] Marx painted a thoroughly idyllic image of that Paris spring:

> Wonderful, indeed, was the change the Commune had wrought in Paris! No longer any trace of the meretricious Paris of the Second Empire. No longer was Paris the

rendezvous of British landlords, Irish absentees, American ex-slaveholders and shoddy men, Russian ex-serfowners, and Wallachian boyards. No more corpses at the morgue, no nocturnal burglaries, scarcely any robberies; in fact, for the first time since the days of February 1848, the streets of Paris were safe, and that without any police of any kind.[9]

'Working, thinking, fighting, bleeding' Paris was 'radiant in the enthusiasm of its historical initiative!'[10] It was, however, forgetful of the 'cannibals' at the city gates. Marx placed the ferocity of the repression squarely at the feet of the Thiers government, which had conducted a civil war under the patronage of a foreign invader.

Marx concluded that the world had changed utterly: 'After Whit-Sunday 1871, there can be neither peace nor truce possible between the working men of France and the appropriators of their produce ... And the French working class is only the advanced guard of the modern proletariat.'[11] This fine essay ended with a ringing call for revenge: 'Working men's Paris, with its Commune, will be for ever celebrated as the glorious harbinger of a new society. Its martyrs are enshrined in the great heart of the working class. Its exterminators' history is already nailed to that eternal pillory from which all the prayers of their priests will not avail to redeem them.'[12]

In his 1891 introduction to *The Civil War in France*, Friedrich Engels described the Mur des Fédérés as 'a mute but eloquent testimony to the frenzy of which the ruling class is capable as soon as the working class dares to stand up for its rights'.[13] The Parisian 'working class', by introducing universal suffrage and the right of recall of representatives who earned a worker's wage, effected a 'shattering' of the former state power and its replacement by a new and truly democratic one. It was enough to terrify the bourgeoisie and its lukewarm critics: 'Of late, the Social-Democratic philistine has once more been filled with wholesome terror at the words: Dictatorship of the Proletariat. Well and good, gentlemen, do you want to know what this dictatorship looks like? Look at the Paris Commune. That was the Dictatorship of the Proletariat.'[14]

Of course, the Marxist interpretation of the Commune can be strongly contested: the revival of a Paris Commune, of the journal *Le Père Duchêne*, and the creation, in the dying weeks, of a Committee of Public Safety, suggest that, if anything, the 1871 Commune was the last hurrah of Parisian sansculottism; a failed re-enactment of the Jacobin Terror of 1793–94. It was anachronistic to describe as working-class a revolt where bohemia, as well as artisans, played a key role. The experiments in direct democracy and federalism could lend themselves to a more liberal or libertarian interpretation. Even the far right could appropriate the anti-German patriotism of the rebels. At the same time, for moderate republicans, there was the issue of the Commune refusing to accept the democratic verdict of France as a whole. What's more, towards the end of his life, Marx himself was privately critical of the Communards, regretting their inability to negotiate a compromise with Versailles.

Nevertheless, the Marxist view of the Commune, as a first attempt at establishing the 'Dictatorship of the Proletariat', gained traction and become a central reference for Lenin's Bolsheviks. According to Marian Sawer, 'it was extremely important to the early Bolshevik leaders that their revolution should be viewed as the direct descendant (via the 1905 Revolution) of the Paris Commune, rather than as the descendant of, for example, the Pugachev rebellion. While native antecedents were not completely ignored, the lineal descent from 1789, 1793 and 1871 was attributed far greater importance. The genealogy of the Russian Revolution was to be European rather than Russian, in support of its universalist aspirations.'[15] They did not want to pass for Asiatic terrorists, 'Blanquists with Tartar sauce'.

For Lenin, Trotsky and other Bolsheviks, the new Soviet regime had learned the lessons of the Commune's failure and was finally fulfilling the Communards' dreams. It is no surprise that, according to legend, in early 1918, an otherwise austere Lenin was seen dancing in the snow to celebrate his regime outliving that of 1871. The 18 March was immediately instituted as a national holiday, while the walls of Leningrad, Moscow and other cities and villages of Russia were plastered with posters depicting the scenes of the Commune, in particular the executions of Bloody Week, and pointing out their moral lesson.

In pamphlets such as Lenin's *State and Revolution* and Trotsky's *Defence of Terrorism*, the Bolsheviks analysed the strengths and weaknesses of the Commune. As their masters Marx and Engels had pointed out, the Communards smashed the bourgeois state, instituted untrammelled workers' power, and took on the priesthood, those 'gendarmes in cassocks'. However, they noted, the Communards had not displayed the steely discipline of the Bolsheviks in Petrograd. They had shown excessive respect for legality and property: they had refused to seize the Bank of France and to march on Versailles, and lacked a clear-cut programme. For Lenin and Trotsky, a disciplined vanguard party and a good dose of 'Red Terror' were necessary to defeat the descendants of Thiers. Thus the lessons of the Paris Commune drew a thick red line between the hard-headed Third International and the 'opportunistic' illusions peddled by social-democrats such as Karl Kautsky and Léon Blum, who thought it possible to win power peacefully through the ballot box.

The link between 1871 and 1917 was made clear in 1924, after the premature death of Lenin. On 24 May, the PCF section of the 20th arrondissement decided to hand over the flag of the 67th Battalion of the Paris Commune to the Moscow Soviet. Although the French government refused the Bellevillois the right to travel, the flag was taken by the PCF delegation to the 5th Congress of the Comintern, which displayed it at a grandiose demonstration attended by an estimated 400,000 people. The flag was brandished again on the occasion of the tenth anniversary of the outbreak of the First World War and the assassination of socialist leader Jean Jaurès. It was then carried inside the makeshift wooden Lenin mausoleum that stood in Red Square.

The French and Soviet Communists therefore both staked a big claim on the heritage of the Paris Commune. In fact, the October Revolution only served to widen the gaps between the various organisations that kept the memory of the Commune alive. Also in 1924, the PCF called on its militants to come (often in military uniform) to Père-Lachaise 'to reconquer the streets, to bring down the regime of exploitation and war, to prepare the Red Day, to commemorate our elder brothers, to defend the Commune.'[16]

In the face of this, the reformist SFIO led by Léon Blum presented itself as the guardian of traditions that were being violated and hastened to denounce Communist 'hijacking' of the pilgrimage to the Wall. In 1926, the PCF invited its *frère-ennemi* to turn the commemoration into a demonstration against fascism and the war in Morocco, and for wage increases. The SFIO leadership retorted that this would detract from what was simply a demonstration by the Paris proletariat in honour of its glorious dead. Indeed, it can be said that this period saw a dwindling of the Communard 'memory' proper, as Communards aged and died. Elderly Fédérés even found themselves jostled aside at the Wall by PCF militants.[17]

The PCF archives give us an idea of the Bolshevik reading of the Commune, adopted by the French with all its Leninist panoply. On 6 March 1926, the agitprop section of the central committee circulated a memo to regional secretaries and 'all agitators'. It instructed them that 'a Proletarian Revolution does not break out at a date fixed a long time in advance; it is the crowning point of a sometimes long, sometimes short, period when the class struggle becomes amplified.' This depended on the activity of the revolutionary proletariat, its ability to lead the masses to fight, and to direct their action. This proletariat had to know how to make a 'correct analysis' of the political situation, in order not to miss the historical moment when the working class should move from defence to attack. It also had to be capable of 'keeping the initiative that allows it to outmanoeuvre the counter-attacks of the Bourgeoisie', and thus ensure the Revolution's victory. This had to be properly understood so that, from the analysis of the revolt that was the Commune, a lesson could be drawn on 'how to avoid recreating the errors made and how to avenge the Fédérés of 28 May 1871, through a Victorious Commune'.

According to the memorandum, the Communards had lacked the strict discipline of the Third International. There was no central organisation, while the Central Committee of the National Guard were masked behind an appearance of concern for legality, 'its fear of responsibilities'. The Communards ran into trouble due to their own fears of legality, which could only weaken them in the face of a bourgeoisie determined to use all the resources at its disposal. In addition, the Commune suffered from '*a lack of links with the exterior*', that is, with both the French peasantry and foreign countries. It also lacked a taste for dictatorship: Thiers attacked by means of 'the White Terror, while the Communards did not organise the Red Terror'. Some '36,000' workers were massacred and, at the Mur des Fédérés, the last Communards 'expiated the crime of having tried to liberate the proletariat from the yoke of the French bourgeoisie'.

It was in Russia that these deaths were avenged. 'In 1917, the Commune triumphed in Leningrad. All that the Paris Commune lacked, the Russian Revolution possessed: an organised Revolutionary party, capable of taking energetic decisions and above all not hobbling itself with a vague and debilitating petit-bourgeois idealism.' Hence this conclusion by Agit-Prop:

The Communists, on the occasion of the anniversary of the Commune, are saying to the workers: 'You must organise to defend yourselves. You must be unionised and promote unity. You must come with us, not only to learn to become good revolutionaries, but also to defend yourselves and achieve your immediate demands. You must unify your action against the bourgeoisie. This is indispensable for the struggles you will face tomorrow. And if, when the moment comes, you are not in a position to oppose your bloc of forces against the united bloc of capitalism, then we will perhaps see the Commune of '71, but will certainly not have the commune of the Bolsheviks of 1917, a proletarian victory.[18]

However, it seems that this message hardly touched the French masses. On 30 May 1929, the Party's Section for Social Organisation deplored the passivity and pessimism reigning in the Paris region, but noted nonetheless: 'At the Wall, we had workers who have struggled against repression. We must call on them to reinforce our regional committee. These combative elements will create a new atmosphere in the committee.'[19] The struggle therefore continued to impose a Cominternist meaning on the Commune, against social democracy and anarchism (and implicitly against the theses of Marx himself on the withering away of the state). In 1931, at the sixtieth anniversary of the Commune, Agit-Prop decided:

In the light of these experiences and that of the Russian Revolution we must clarify more precisely the following questions: the necessity of the Party (recruitment), the dictatorship of the proletariat (USSR), and the uncompromising struggle against the bourgeoisie (class against class).

For Agit-Prop, it was necessary to propagate the conclusions of Lenin:

Despite universal [male] suffrage, the Commune did not represent from the beginning all the classes of the capital's population and was not, in large part, a democratic general assembly, but an organ created by the Paris proletariat. Its aims were:

To break the bourgeois state

To arm the people

The separation of Church and State

'Social-fascists' such as Karl Kautsky, with their opposition to a 'premature' seizure of power, and attachment to the concept of securing a parliamentary majority, had disowned the Commune. At the same time, however, the great masses of the West had noticed, before and after the war, how 'democracy' 'stifle[d] any revolutionary movement'; how thus democracy became 'the assassin of Karl Liebknecht, Rosa Luxemburg and tens of thousands of revolutionary workers'; how 'today, with the full support of fascism, it murders workers in broad daylight, outlaws Communist parties, introduces medieval forms of torture in prisons and actively arms itself for war.' On the sixtieth anniversary of the Paris Commune, the masses in their thousands would 'brandish its flag under the slogan of struggle for Soviet power, for the World Commune.'

The sectarian politics of the PCF, and its reading of the Commune, were illustrated at the death of Zéphirin Camélinat in March 1932, aged ninety-two. The demise of the former finance delegate of the Commune coincided virtually to the day with that of Aristide Briand. Briand, a former foreign minister and fixture in French centre-left politics, had led the way in reviving Franco–German relations as well as building alliances further east to contain the Soviet threat. The funeral processions in Paris for Briand and Camélinat highlighted a bitter political divide. 'To them the renegade, to us the Communard!' exclaimed *L'Humanité*. While Briand was a strike-breaking, anti-Soviet warmonger, Camélinat had been a founder member of the Parisian sections of the First International as well as the PCF, and had played a crucial role in protecting *L'Humanité* from the 'social-patriots' and 'social-traitors' led by Léon Blum.

Against the backdrop of Japanese threats to the Soviet Union and a violent election campaign in moribund Weimar Germany, 120,000 workers marched through Belleville in homage to 'the most faithful and oldest member of the Party', who had insisted he be carried in a pauper's hearse. Marcel Cachin wrote of his 'example': 'His beard and his hair were snow-white. But the face, right to the end, remained young like a heart.'[20]

This reading of the Commune persisted in the PCF plans, in 1933, to mark the fiftieth anniversary of the death of Karl Marx. It was imperative to show, in Leninist fashion, the necessity of a strongly centralised party on a firm ideological basis. On this point, a particular effort would be made 'in our regions still infected by anarcho-syndicalism, such as Paris and Lyon-St Etienne'. The role of Marx and Engels regarding the Commune and the creation and development of Jules Guesde's French Workers' Party, their struggle on the two fronts in the French and international workers' movement, had to be widely disseminated while also pointing out the 'primordial mistakes' made by Guesde and Lafargue, which had led to the 'opportunistic degeneration' of Guesdism in the final years of the nineteenth century and 'which still strongly impregnate our region in the Nord, particularly in trade union work and its contempt for anti-militarist work.'

The Party therefore decided to republish the *Communist Manifesto* as well as Marx's *Civil War in France*. A special brochure on the Commune contained the views of Marx, Engels, Lenin and Stalin on the event. The narrative showed that the USSR had put Marx's theory into concrete practice, through a dictatorship of the proletariat. Other articles looked at wars and critiqued petit-bourgeois pacifism; the unity of the working class; the situation and particular role of the peasantry; and the national and colonial question, applied concretely to Alsace-Lorraine and the French colonies. Marx's indications concerning socialist society, and the realisation of those indications in the USSR, 'unmasked' the petit-bourgeois and anti-socialist character of the 'egalitarian' redistribution presented by socialist and anarchist demagogy as the criterion for socialism. Finally, the brochure looked at the struggle against religion, which 'must enable us, with Marxist conceptions, to rigorously fight the theories developed in 1929 at the SFIO Congress in Nancy'. This part 'must be dealt with by the fraction of the Association of Proletarian Freethinkers'.[21] Thus the PCF continued in the republican tradition of intransigent anti-clericalism to which Lejeune, and many others, had adhered before 1871.

In May 1933, the magazine *Regards* brought out a special issue, *Vive la Commune!* The front cover was dominated by Marx, Engels and Lenin, while inside, images and text juxtaposed the Paris Commune and the October Revolution. Thus, Théophile Ferré, the delegate responsible for General

Security, was placed alongside Felix Dzerzhinsky, chief of the Cheka, then the NKVD. A drawing of the Central Committee of the National Guard putting down the bourgeois uprising of 22 March 1871 faced a photograph of Tsarist generals being arrested by Red Guards. A portrait of the Commune's Hungarian minister of labour, Léo Frankel, was accompanied by images of a Soviet metal-workers' rest home and workers and peasants sitting the entrance exam for the Workers' Faculty of the Institute of Mechanics. There were photographs of old Bolsheviks like Sverdlov, and frequently Stalin (but certainly no Trotsky). The women of the Commune, notably Louise Michel, were present, alongside Lenin's widow Krupskaya and Elena Stasova, former Party secretary and now president of International Red Aid, the MOPR. The heroic Polish generals Wroblewski and Dombrowski found their contemporary equivalent in Voroshilov, commander of the Red Army.

The Commune may have been defeated in Paris, then, but it had triumphed in the USSR. In his article on 'The Essential Lesson of the Commune', PCF leader André Marty still trained fire on the 'social-traitor' rival, despite the recent catastrophe in Germany: 'By supporting a government which has not fulfilled a single one of its electoral promises, and thus sows bitter disillusionment among the workers, is the SFIO not also actively helping fascism?'[22]

We therefore see, in this memorialising of the Commune, a Communist Party viscerally attached to a USSR that was increasingly held in Stalin's steel fist; hostile to parliamentary democracy, sectarian towards the rest of the French left, and violently anti-clerical (at this time the Communists had an organisation inspired by the Republican Association of Freethinkers, the 'Godless Workers'). We are still in the Comintern's 'Third Period' of 'class against class', imposing a merciless struggle against the 'social-fascism' embodied by the SFIO. The Popular Front, with its 'outstretched hand' to Christians, a 'Socialism in the Colours of France', and therefore a patriotic Paris Commune, did not yet exist. Clearly, the supposed autobiography of Lejeune, published in 1931, was completely in line with this world view.

In 1922, Adrien Lejeune joined the French Section of the Communist International. His eyes, like those of his comrades, were turned towards the 'light in the East'. But the date of his departure for the USSR has been disputed. In 1940, André Marty wrote: 'Lejeune has always been extremely faithful to the working class. When, in 1928, on the initiative of International Red Aid, he was sent to the USSR, he handed over his entire "fortune" in stocks and bonds to Marcel Cachin, Director of *L'Humanité* (35,000 francs).' According to *France-URSS*: '1924: at the Mausoleum, Lenin lay beneath a flag from the barricades of Belleville, perhaps a flag in the shadow of which Adrien fought fifty-three years earlier. Increasingly, Adrien Lejeune, the old Communard, regarded the Soviet Union as his second homeland, and in 1926, he decided to leave France for the USSR. In the spring of 1926, Adrien Lejeune arrived in Moscow where he was greeted by veterans of the Revolution. He was seventy-nine years old.'[23] The venerable 'Maitron', biographical dictionary of the French labour movement, gives 1928 as the date of departure, and *L'Humanité* 1926.

Lejeune's personal file, in the Moscow archives, allows us to dismiss both these dates. It informs us of a tragic detail in the Communard's private life. Lejeune had indeed ended up finding a wife, late in life; he married Jeanne Augustine Pichon at the *mairie* of the 11th arrondissement on 4 February 1913. Their wedded bliss proved brief. On 15 December 1926, Madame Lejeune died in their home in Draveil, south-east of Paris, at the age of fifty, and was buried in the local cemetery: 'no flowers by request'.

Lejeune had left Bagnolet for Draveil well before the Great War: he was in this small town in 1908, when Prime Minister Georges Clemenceau sent in troops to break a quarrymen's strike, causing several fatalities and striking a deadly blow at revolutionary syndicalism. Three years later in Draveil, the ex-Communard Paul Lafargue and his wife Laura Marx injected themselves with cyanide to escape the ordeal of 'pitiless old age'. There is no evidence, however, of any contact between this couple and Lejeune.

The death of Lejeune's wife might have motivated a departure for the USSR in 1926, but not in such a precipitate manner. As for 1928, this date is refuted by a photograph of

Adrien Lejeune (seated, far right) alongside
other Commune veterans (Paris, 1929)

the last survivors of the Commune at the traditional Parisian banquet in May 1929, where we see a smiling Lejeune. The following document in the file gives us the true date of departure. It records Lejeune's decision 'to hand over to *L'Humanité* 4,626 francs of annuity. These securities become the property for the New Society of the newspaper *L'Humanité* from this day onward, on condition that the said society ensures me an annual income corresponding to that yielded by my securities'. The document is signed and dated: 'Paris, 22 May 1930'.

After his departure for Moscow, which took place after the anniversary of the Bloody Week, Lejeune received a letter from the newspaper's administrator, Edouard Cormon, which gives us an idea of the pecuniary demands of the old Communard in the context of deepening European crisis:

> I'm going to see with the board of directors what it is possible to do with your 4,600 francs of stocks. ... That said, I want to point out to you that I am not lazy as you say and I have not received any letter from you since your departure ... I saw some very interesting things in Germany but I assure you that I would have liked to push my journey further and go to shake your hand in your new but genuine homeland. I think that you are having a good time there and have good comrades to keep you company.

4

Lejeune in the USSR

In September 1930, Lejeune was warmly thanked by a MOPR official, who wrote: 'I acknowledge receipt of the 2000 francs you send me and thank you wholeheartedly. Your gesture is worthy of a combatant of the Paris Commune who has remained faithful to the cause of the proletariat. I have transferred the 2000 francs to the Red Aid fund devoted to alleviating the lot of political prisoners and their families.'

In Lejeune's correspondence we detect a mixture of militancy and pragmatic materialism. On 21 October 1930, *L'Humanité* wrote to 'Comrade Lejeune', residing at the Home for Old Bolsheviks, in Moscow:

[Your letter] brings good news from you and shows that your morale is more than excellent. I agree completely that the socialists can hardly feel 'satisfied' with their 'victory' in Belleville; they have now been reduced to using any means to struggle against Communism. As for us, our campaign was excellent and despite the fact that [Maurice] Thorez was not elected, we are very happy with the result. The contribution of 80 francs to *L'Humanité* instead of Red Aid was a small error which is easily rectified. We will send you the coffee and chocolate, and all that you ask for in the letter.

This correspondent gives a rather rose-tinted image of the heavy defeat for the PCF's general secretary in the former Communard stronghold of the 20th arrondissement. These poor results were severely criticised by the Comintern and followed by a shake-up at the top of the French Party.

Curiously absent from the surviving correspondence at this time is the Communists' conquest of the municipality of Bagnolet. Since the end of the nineteenth century, the village had changed beyond recognition, with the establishment of wood, metal and glue manufacturers there. The *croquants* and their orchards were wiped out by industrialisation, while the radicalised workers who replaced them would make of Bagnolet, until as late as 2014, one of the bastions of the 'Red Belt'.

In 1931, Lejeune received 50 roubles from the MOPR for his manuscript of 'memoirs'. Also in that year, Elena Stasova, the organisation's president, wrote him a letter of thanks for the generous donation he had made to help 'revolutionary militants who have fallen victim to White Terror and Fascism'. Those 31,000 francs, she said, represented what he had been 'obliged to save with difficulty throughout an entire working life in order to benefit from it in old age. But today, to you the old combatant of seventy-one, the former convict abused by Versaillais reaction, the Proletarian Revolution gives hospitality and guarantees you a better old age than the one afforded by savings made under the capitalist regime'.

For Stasova, Lejeune had been a pioneer of the revolutionary movement, who struggled to defend the first attempt at workers' government made by the Communards; indeed, 'the beaten Commune was not vanquished, for since Red October until today it has continued victorious.' Now that he was in the USSR, Lejeune could see 'that for which you fought in your youth and for which you have devoted all your life as a militant: the workers' and peasants' state, Socialist Society'. His 'magnificent' donation brought succour to the victims of the revolutionary struggle, but it was also 'a sign of trust in the Revolutionary Homeland, in the construction of socialism of which you can admire the victorious march'. Finally, it constituted 'an example and an appeal to the workers of the entire world, and in particular the workers of France who must struggle against French imperialism, rampart of world counter-revolution'.

That said, in the course of the 1930s, as the 'brown beast' of fascism became ever more menacing, Lejeune's messages to Paris seem to have been largely focused on material demands. On 7 September 1933, months after Adolf Hitler had taken power, *L'Humanité* wrote to Moscow: 'We acknowledge receipt of your letter asking for a sum of 2,000 to 3,000 francs. You are well aware of the exchange problems which sadly will not allow us to send you so rapidly the sum requested; nevertheless, we will strive to satisfy you.' On 6 December 1933, another missive attempted to reassure him:

You asked comrade Sandberg to procure for you, in Paris, a whole series of objects. We have hastened to give this comrade all the facilities and possibilities she needed to make the purchases requested. We are convinced that you will be very pleased when comrade Sandberg delivers the various small items you wanted … Our wish is that you should keep in excellent health for a long time, our old Communard who remains one of the last living symbols of the Paris Commune.

In light of all this, it does not seem that the veteran was badly treated. Stasova wrote to him in November 1934: 'I am very glad that you had a pleasant journey and that you have had a good rest in the sanatorium in the Caucasus. I hope that you have gathered enough strength to comfortably bear the winter in Moscow.'

But this living symbol was voracious. In December 1934, around the time of the assassination of Leningrad party boss Kirov, Lejeune heard as follows from Paris: 'You know, life at *l'Humanité* is not without difficulties, we often have trouble paying our bills; a seasoned militant like yourself is sufficiently aware of all these issues for us not to have to insist on them any more.' All the same, the comrades did their best: 'We send you warmest wishes for the New Year. Our comrade is bringing you a few treats: 2 bottles of wine, 2 bars of chocolate, some pears, 2 tins of sardines, some biscuits, as well as some pocket money.' In July 1935, Lejeune was reassured that '*L'Humanité* bears no hard feelings towards you.'

Indeed, on the symbolic level, Lejeune had increasing importance for the Cause. Cachin and Marty would soon be in Moscow for the Seventh (and final) Congress of the Comintern, which would decide upon the new line of a 'Popular Front' against fascism; the two leaders planned to drop in on Lejeune. His old Communard comrades in Moscow were now dead: the songwriter Achille Leroy, who had been invited in October 1927 to the festivities of the tenth anniversary of the Russian Revolution, died in Moscow in 1929 (despite his expressed wish to return to Paris). That year also saw the death of Henri Fourcade, another Communard who had been living in the USSR for some years. In 1935, with the passing of the poet Gustave Hinard, Lejeune seemed to be the last Communard left. This was not entirely true: still alive in France were Emile Chausse (born in 1850) and Pierre Vidal (born in 1851); but Chausse was a long-standing socialist councillor in Paris, and Vidal had quit politics at the end of the nineteenth century, after a period of exile in Hungary and Romania. Neither man fitted the narrative demanded by the Comintern (and both would die in 1941, before Lejeune).

As an illustration of Lejeune's new symbolic importance, in September 1935 he was one of those who paid their last respects to the open coffin of the novelist Henri Barbusse, who was abruptly taken ill after a visit to the Moscow Zoo. Much was made of the premature disappearance of the author of *Under Fire*, one of the most eminent of the French intellectuals then promoting the notion of an anti-fascist 'popular front'. In the great hall of the Moscow Conservatory, his guard of honour included Nikolai Bulganin, president of the Moscow Soviet, Nikita Khrushchev, Elena Stasova and American Communist leader Earl Browder. The journalist Alexander Koltsov paid homage to his French colleague. According to *L'Humanité*, after 'hundreds of thousands' of Muscovite workers had reverently filed past the coffin, there remained only 'the closest friends: a delegation of the Central Committee of the PCF, led by Thorez and Marty; a delegation of Young Communists from France led by Raymond Guyot; the delegation of French Communists living in Moscow. Among them could be made out the old Communard, comrade Lejeune.'[1]

The coffin was transported from Moscow, via Pilsudski's Poland and Hitler's Germany, to Père-Lachaise, thus inaugurating this Communist enclave in the cemetery. In *Monde*, the international weekly founded by Barbusse, François Beaupréau described the coffin's welcome: 'The crowd of Paris, the real Paris, enters the great cemetery. And everyone's thoughts associate the Wall with Barbusse ... Along the walls of Père-Lachaise, the endless queue stretches out like a fresco, where all the labouring classes, all the disinherited and all men of courage and hope are represented. ... Union! Liberty! Peace!'[2]

From now on, as the Last Communard, Lejeune carried on his ageing shoulders an important and prestigious responsibility – even though a representative of the Friends of the Commune, Valette, wrote to him in October 1935: 'Dear friend Lejeune, the letter of 1931 addressed to the nursing home in Petrolovska near Moscow was returned to me with the comment: "unknown"! We would be very happy if you could, for the Museum of the Commune, send us your news and your memoirs.'

But what explains the sometimes tense exchanges between Lejeune and *L'Humanité*, the newspaper founded by Jaurès and once under the patronage of Camélinat? Were these just the – completely human and understandable – caprices of an extremely old man (especially for a worker born in 1847)? Or did his incessant demands hide a slightly darker reality?

Once in the USSR, Lejeune had come under the protection

of André Marty, son of a veteran of the Narbonne Commune who had been condemned to death *in absentia*. A hero of the Black Sea mutiny in 1919, Marty became secretary of the Comintern in France and political commissar of the International Brigades in Spain (for which he earned the sobriquet 'the butcher of Albacete'). In December 1940, now serving as one of the PCF's exiled leadership and tasked in Moscow with looking after the welfare of the Last Communard, Marty wrote appreciatively:

> Lejeune is one of the last true fighters of the Paris Commune ... He has always taken part in the revolutionary workers' movement, organised for a period in the revolutionary social-ist party of [Edouard] Vaillant. During the first imperialist war Lejeune, already very old, violently denounced the socialists' participation in government and support for the war. From the very beginning he was on the side of the October Revolution.

Because of his long-standing admiration for the Last Communard, Marty had become exasperated by the old man's situation, and, as early as 1935, wrote a 'Note on the situation of comrade Adrien Lejeune, former Communard'. Here it transpired that given the donation of his securities to *L'Humanité*, it had been agreed in the course of 1932 between comrade Lejeune, the managers of MOPR and Marty that:

> 1) a – All that comrade Lejeune asks for, of whatever nature, will be immediately given to him (food, for example, wine, chocolate, etc), and if the purchases must be made in *valuta* [hard currency], they will be made in *valuta*.

b – The Directorate of the MOPR is charged with applying this decision.

2) To my knowledge, this decision has always been applied; regular visits are made to Lejeune by officials of the MOPR.

3) This decision has been made because comrade Adrien Lejeune has been continually surrounded by old women whose sole aim is to sponge off the old Communard. Currently he has next to him a woman who gives herself the title of former wife of the Communard Hinard, who died in Moscow about two years ago [sic]. She is a woman from Odessa, and it is she who is always pushing 'father' Lejeune to ask for his money.

If, Marty continued, the PCF was ready to do anything for comrade Lejeune, 'it is not ready to give money to an adventuress who has scandalously been allowed to latch onto the old Communard.' Since '1928', this woman 'has not ceased to make the most insolent requests of the PCF's representatives in Moscow'. Her very letter indicated her state of mind. It was completely false to say that comrade Lejeune had to pay special fees for personnel and hospitalisation: he was at the Kremlin hospital and all his expenses were covered by the MOPR. It was clear that the person who wrote the letter 'has always had one essential goal: to have money, not to improve the situation of old Lejeune but for her personal interests, which have nothing to do with the revolutionary workers' movement'.

Just a month previously, she had caused a 'violent scandal' by declaring that Cachin and Marty 'went to the theatre every evening in Moscow and could not be bothered to go and see

Lejeune'. On the basis of previous decisions, it was shortly to be verified whether Lejeune had indeed continued to receive what he requested. In Marty's opinion, the only response to make to comrade Lejeune was to 'continue to give him all he desires, whatever the demands he makes, but measures must be taken not to enrich at our expense the adventuresses prowling around him'. We know nothing more about these ladies.

Throughout this uneasy time of vigilance and suspicion, the French Communists continued to supply the Last Communard. On 3 December 1935, the chief administrator of *L'Humanité* wrote to announce the immediate despatch of 2,000 francs. On 17 July 1936, Lejeune was promised that a delegation of the Friends of the USSR would 'bring a parcel containing all the objects you asked for'. On 13 September 1936, as Stalin's Terror extended its grasp in Moscow and beyond, one comrade Planque wrote: 'I have therefore bought for you: 3 flannel shirts; 4 pairs of woollen socks; 2 cotton bonnets; 2 sponges; to which I shall add half a kilo of chocolate and as much coffee, to be sent Monday morning. I will also include the glass and rubber tubes.' But only a month later, the correspondent at *L'Humanité* sighed: 'We are very upset by the comments in your letter, for you know perfectly well that we do all we can to satisfy all your requests.' A few weeks later again, Planque had more comforting news: 'In a few days' time a delegation will leave here for the 19th anniversary of the October Revolution. I hope to contact one of the comrades of this delegation and will ask him to bring you a few delicacies from the great Paris of the Commune, which made so many capitalist bandits tremble sixty-five years ago.' Planque therefore remained a good friend. On 26 April 1937, he wrote:

'[Comrade Villiot] will bring you two bottles of wine, two bars of chocolate, a box of dates, a few bananas and a small coffee filter-machine, enough for a cup. Oh *damn*! I notice I've forgotten the coffee!!! How absent-minded I am.'

This eminent old Communard could be exasperating, but his very existence had to be celebrated. On 3 June 1937, to mark Lejeune's ninetieth birthday, Marcel Cachin and Paul Vaillant-Couturier wrote to him in the name of *L'Humanité*:

It is with joy that we wish, on this occasion, to express the sympathy of all the comrades at *L'Humanité*, happy in the knowledge that you are in good health despite your advanced age, and feel surrounded by the affection and concern of our brothers in the Land of Socialism. We know that you follow as ardently as ever the struggles and successes of our Communist Party and the Popular Front in France. We are sure that you rejoice in the immense progress achieved by our Party, which bring to you in old age the revenge for the difficult struggles you waged in the past. What better wish could we send, Dear Comrade, on the occasion of your birthday, than that you may for many years yet admire the gigantic achievements of victorious Socialism in the Land of the Soviets, and that you may witness, in our country, the triumph of the cause to which you have devoted your long and courageous life as a proletarian militant.

There were also elogious messages from the Friends of the USSR, the Communist parliamentary group, and this one from the MOPR, couched in the language of those Stalinist times:

We wish you long life, dear Adrien Lejeune, in our happy, joyful and prosperous Soviet land. We sincerely wish you live long enough to see the total victory of the working class over the fascist beast, and see with your own eyes the victorious flag of the Paris Commune fly over every country.

Long live the veteran of the Paris Commune, Adrien Lejeune!

Long live the heroic proletariat struggling against fascism!

Long live the Great Socialist State of workers and peasants!

Long live the home of the world socialist revolution and the Third Communist International!

Long live the Communist Party under the Great Leader of Nations, comrade Stalin!

Marty also wrote to Lejeune of the 'living symbol of the implacable struggle of the proletariat and people of Paris against the exploiters'. He concluded: 'While we wait to receive you in our liberated Paris, may you, the undefeated combatant from the last barricade, on the rue des Pyrénées, receive, dear comrade Lejeune, my most cordial, fraternal and revolutionary congratulations.' In the context of the Spanish Civil War, where Marty was carving out his own brutal reputation as a paranoid and ruthless political commissar of the International Brigades, the choice of a barricade in the rue des Pyrénées was all the more symbolic.

Meanwhile the struggle to satisfy the hero of the Commune continued. A letter of 26 October 1937 began by speaking of the 'objects' requested by Lejeune, before announcing 'the terrible death of our comrade [Paul] Vaillant-Couturier': the youthful director of *L'Humanité* would be buried a few metres from the tomb of Barbusse. On 7 December 1937, it was nervously explained that a comrade who was to bring Lejeune more stuff had fallen ill: 'We are sure you will not be angry with us for this small delay outside our control. You know how much the life of a newspaper is full of unpredictable events of all kinds, and we hope the parcel you receive will please you.' But despite these efforts, the newspaper had to grovel to him four days later: 'We are very upset by your remarks suggesting that we have neglected to do the favour you asked of us, and we hope that after receiving this letter, you will no longer be angry with us.' On 12 January 1938, the hapless Planque tried to put these minor contretemps into perspective: 'You'll have read about our great victory at Teruel! If our Spanish Comrades could buy the weapons they need, this war would quickly be over with the defeat of Franco and a stunning victory for the Republican Armies. But despite all that, their victory is certain.'

In Lejeune's files in Moscow, there is no mention of any gift to the children of Spanish Republicans. That said, the Soviet journalist Alexander Kukhno, in an article published in 1967 in *Literaturnaya Gazeta*, asserts that Lejeune did make a gesture of solidarity towards the Republicans: 'In 1937–1938, the Communard Lejeune, aged ninety, followed with great concern and anxiety the events unfolding in Spain, constantly asking for news of those who took part in the first battles against the fascists. He asked for news of the Spanish children at [the home] Simiaza. He gave his last savings to the MOPR.'[3] According to Kukhno, it was at the sanatorium of Barvikha that Lejeune made the acquaintance of Isidoro Acevedo, a writer from Asturias born in 1876, co-founder of the Spanish

Communist Party, who had organised hospitals on the front line as well as the evacuation to the USSR of the children of Republicans.

But despite the tireless efforts of the comrades at *L'Humanité*, and this new friendship with Acevedo, Lejeune did not perhaps feel completely at home in the Land of the Soviets. On 13 June 1938, in a confidential report to comrade Andreyev of the Executive Committee of the Comintern, Bogdanov, chief of the Central Committee of the MOPR, wrote:

> We do not know where you get the information that the old Communard Lejeune died two years ago. At that time he resided in the Ilyich Home in Moscow before being transferred to the sanatorium at Mikhailovskoye. At present he is in the Kremlin clinic and will return to Mikhailovskoye in a few days' time. Given there are no French comrades in the MOPR, we ask you to ensure that French comrades come to visit him. Mikhailovskoye is sixty kilometres from the city and sometimes he feels very lonely.

On 29 October 1938, in an 'urgent and confidential' letter, Bogdanov wrote again to Andreyev, insisting he arrange for members of the French and Spanish delegations to the October anniversary celebrations to visit Lejeune in his sanatorium:

> In the past, delegates always visited him, yet the delegation that came for the 1 May celebrations did not make the journey, which greatly disappointed comrade Lejeune. What's more the Central Committee of the MOPR of the USSR request

that you make sure that the Spanish delegates led by Morato, currently residing at the Savoy Hotel, visit comrade Lejeune.

Despite these difficulties and disappointments, tributes were still paid to the Last Communard. After the defeat of the Spanish Republic, Edouard Chenel, secretary for the Fraternal Association of Veterans and Friends of the Paris Commune, asked him to autograph his menu for the banquet of May 1939. On 1 May 1939, comrade Lejeune – 'heroic participant in the immortal Commune!' – received the homage of his companions at the sanatorium of Barvikha.

Indeed, Lejeune and many Russians he encountered could count themselves lucky. Of those who had paid homage to Henri Barbusse in September 1935, Nikolai Bulganin survived the Great Terror and would enjoy a long political career well beyond the end of the Second World War. Elena Stasova, despite her courageously outspoken defence of some victims of Stalinist repression, would also prosper. But this contrasted cruelly with the fate of the journalist Mikhail Kolstov, Stalin's special correspondent in Spain, who was arrested for his pains and shot in 1940. In the last great show trial of the Terror, the 'doctors' trial', the unfortunate accused were implicated in the death not only of Maxim Gorky, but of Barbusse himself. Paradoxically, Barbusse's hagiography of Stalin had long since been withdrawn from the shelves, just as many of the Great Leader's 'friends and companions', notably Karl Radek, had themselves fallen into disgrace.

The year of 1939 brought new crises for the Communist movement. After the rout of the Spanish Republicans, and in the face of the equivocations of Franco–British diplomacy,

Stalin signed a non-aggression treaty with his erstwhile mortal enemy, Hitler. A friendship pact would follow. According to the new Comintern line, any defensive war waged by the remaining Western democracies would be 'imperialist'. As a consequence of this breakneck U-turn, the French Communist Party was outlawed in its homeland. Its leaders, Thorez, Duclos and Marty, took refuge in the USSR.

As for the Last Communard, he seemed to be in good shape and loyal to the line defined by the party. At the end of 1940, after the calamitous fall of the Third Republic, André Marty described him thus:

> At the current moment, comrade Lejeune continues to follow political events and shows an excellent class spirit. For example, although he cannot read, due to his weakening eyesight, he expresses opinions, on the break-up of the Popular Front, the attitude of the Socialists, of the Daladier government, on the attitude of the Communist deputies, that are absolutely correct and clear ideas; it is even astonishing that, at his age, he has kept such clarity of mind and such a memory. Whilst a certain number of old Communists have passed themselves off as Communards, Lejeune, who fought in the 20th arrondissement on the last barricades, has always been extremely modest in every way.

But behind this flattering report hid a sadder reality, which Marty described to the Comintern in a confidential report. Lejeune was currently in the Kremlin Clinic. For twenty-five days now, the crisis which had required his hospitalisation was over. Despite this, he was still in his sick ward, subject to hospital regulations, in particular those concerning visits. Various organisations continued the discussion about him which had been ongoing for several years. The sanatorium at Barvikha had in fact refused to take him back, because the MOPR had not paid for the last eight months he spent there. At the present time, all expenses were paid, while the MOPR continued to raise the 'eternal Lejeune problem' with the various organisations that might be interested.

Since Marty's opinion had been asked for, he had to point out that it was difficult to justify the treatment of Lejeune. Back in 1928, the Central Committee of the French Communist Party had decided to ask the MOPR if it could take care of the five or six old Communards who were living in France in 'a very bad situation'. On the agreement of the organisations concerned, Lejeune was sent to the USSR with the other comrades. After their death, he had remained alone.

Until around 1936, Marty went on, Lejeune had been installed in the Home for Old Revolutionaries, in Moscow itself. He was very happy there, because other old comrades spoke French; furthermore, the food was quite acceptable. But since 1936 Lejeune had been thrown from one side to another and the MOPR had not settled his situation other than in a strictly administrative way. Lejeune was in an excellent state of health for someone his age. No organ was impaired: he could live 'for another eight or ten years'. His eyesight was deteriorating and his deafness quite pronounced, but the brain was 'excellent'. Nevertheless, Lejeune had lately grown progressively weaker, and Marty suggested two reasons for this. Firstly, there was his permanent isolation in a hospital bedroom:

He hears French spoken, at best, for one hour every ten days. It is difficult in these conditions for bitterness not to invade him and influence his physical state. The only regular visits he receives are those of the French typists, myself, and for two months now [PCF representative] Raymond Guyot. I proposed for example that the MOPR could select groups of Soviet French-speaking comrades from the French language schools in Moscow, and task them with at least fortnightly visits. That would mean two visits *per year* for each group. It has been impossible for me to obtain even a reply to this proposal. When there is a celebration (18 March, 7 November), and the MOPR thinks of it, a delegation goes to visit Lejeune; they smile at one another, shout 'Vive la Commune' and then leave the old comrade all on his own.

Another reason for his ill-health was the fact that comrade Lejeune was 'a French worker. Thus Russian cuisine does not please him any more than German cuisine, and as no one can understand his observations (since the cuisine is different) he hardly eats, and therefore becomes weaker.' No account had been taken of his previous life: 'For example, the French worker drinks wine at every meal; this does not make him a drunkard, for in France, the regions in which wine is not drunk are those that produce the most alcoholics, intoxication being almost unknown in the wine-producing departments of the Midi. Now, Lejeune, as a French worker, would like a bottle of wine from time to time: forbidden!'

Given that nothing had been organised for three or four years to ensure he enjoyed some intellectual and social life, on several occasions he had been surrounded by French-speaking people he naturally trusted, but 'who stole nearly everything he had'. 'Like all French workers', Lejeune liked 'his little personal effects'. Since 1910, he had owned a big watch of little value. In 1939, the glass broke. For three months the MOPR was incapable of replacing the glass, so that old Lejeune no longer knew what time it was and lived 'like a prisoner (or an animal)'. It was Marty who had the watch repaired. A month later Lejeune was taken to hospital, the glass broke again, and no one bothered to have it repaired. Almost all of his cherished personal objects had disappeared. When he asked for a pair of shoes, the MOPR bought him one, but they were so tight that it was torture for him to walk. Everything that might lighten his life was provided 'in an administrative fashion and as if they were doing him a favour [underlined in the original]'.

Marty concluded that 'the best *provisional* solution' for comrade Lejeune would be to house him among veterans of the Revolution, some of whom he knew (there were Italian comrades) and who spoke French. But there would have to be a highly qualified nurse on hand, and '*the possibility of a rapid light surgical intervention when necessary*'. The definitive solution would be, 'as soon as circumstances allow it, his return to France'.

In his post-scriptum, Marty noted angrily that, on the occasion of the 18 March 1940 commemoration, the MOPR had sent one of its officials to visit Lejeune. Immediately afterwards, this official wrote an article entitled 'We Shall Win! On the occasion of the 69th anniversary of the Commune', and signed it 'Adrien Lejeune'. The Press Section of the Communist International let it be printed without even informing Marty.

This article, published in the *Rundschau* (a Comintern organ based in Stockholm), was 'a schematic, lifeless text, full of clichés plus a quotation from Marx'. As could be expected in these febrile times, it was immediately picked up on by the French socialists, in *Le Peuple*, organ of the CGT, on 18 April 1940, who took advantage of it to ridicule Lejeune. Now, after talking it over with him, Marty had proposed an interview under the title 'The Communard Who Saw Three Wars', containing 'only Lejeune's opinions, tidied up, of course, but very lively and very relevant to today'. The problem was that the comrades who 'looked after' Lejeune considered him 'to have regressed to childhood, and they write articles with his signature *that not a single French militant will believe to be by Lejeune*'.

In the *Le Peuple* article, the anonymous socialist journalist laid into the alleged remarks of the Last Communard and his fellow exiles. For him, Lejeune, Thorez and Marty were behaving like 'auxiliaries of Nazi propaganda'. Not much needed to be said about Marty's article; taking the form of a letter to American volunteers in the Spanish Civil War, 'it is a ferocious digression on the "abominable existence" that, according to him, is suffered by the refugees "abandoned" by Blum and Jouhaux, "valets of the French bourgeoisie", "threatened with death every day, every minute". No less than that.' These 'grotesque lies', addressed to a country which had little knowledge of things in Europe, sought to invite the thousands of workers of the New World to come out 'against the unjust and reactionary war' waged by capitalism, in other words to 'take the side of Hitler's Germany, in association with the USSR. Marty has not changed profession.' Thorez's contribution to the same anniversary *Rundschau* issue had an altogether different character, according to *Le Peuple*:

> The 'son of the people' attacks the Communists who had the sense to react against Stalinist policy. The deserter flies into a rage against his former friends whose names we won't please him by citing: N... is a police informer; G..., an informer; V... and G... are opportunists; C..., an arriviste; D..., a failure ... But you can already see a campaign against disillusioned Communists emerge: they are very close to being accused of Trotskyism and to being, in their turn, described as 'lubricious vipers'.

The pick of the bunch was 'a certain Lejeune (André [*sic*]) – has anyone ever heard of him? – who seems to be, in this team, the main one assigned to spreading muck. This individual attacks in particular Blum and Jouhaux, decreed public enemies number 1, in whom are revived the "villains of Versailles", because they are their "despicable descendants", "moral avatars" and a "treacherous rabble." ' In short, 'the escapee from Bobigny or Arcueil has used the anniversary of the Commune as a pretext to unleash his filth. It would be useless to remind him what the Commune was, and what part was played in it by patriotic revolt against the German invader. He is quite incapable of understanding this, since he and his friends recommend and organise treason in the face of the enemy.'[4] By describing Lejeune as an 'escapee' from the red Parisian suburbs of Bobigny or Arcueil was the journalist hinting at an uncomfortable truth, that of Lejeune's relative 'cowardice' during the Bloody Week?

During the uneasy peace between the Comintern and Nazi Germany, the Communist line on the Commune – and therefore the official declarations of the Last Communard – were extremely ambiguous. On the seventieth anniversary of the Commune, in 1941, M. Wolf, secretary of the Comintern Youth, wrote to Lejeune to express the youth section's 'ardent young Communist salutations':

We salute in you those who, seventy years ago, fought heroically on the barricades against counter-revolution, for workers' power, for freedom. Today, because of the Bourgeoisie's treason, the French people is again going through difficult times. But the experience of the glorious Paris Communards taught the French people a great deal and the day is not far off when, guided by the Communist Party, it will rise up against its oppressors and achieve freedom. We hope that you, dear comrade Lejeune, will see the day when the French people will fulfil the dreams of the Paris Communards and build a free and happy Soviet France.

Lejeune replied as follows to his 'young friends':

What a joy it is to see you, the free and strong generation of socialism, the young generation which grows up in the sun of the Stalinist Constitution. Seventy years ago, we, the proletarians of Paris, also tried to overthrow the bourgeoisie and establish working-class power, but we were broken because of our weakness and lack of experience. What we did not succeed in doing has been achieved by the proletariat of Russia under the leadership of the Party of Lenin and Stalin.

So increase the power of the Land of Socialism, absorb the great doctrine of Marx, Engels, Lenin and Stalin, reinforce the international links with the world proletariat. That is the guarantee of future victories. Long live the hope of the workers of the world, the great Stalin![5]

During this strange and tortured period, the Nazis were never directly attacked by the Communists. In June 1940, the PCF leader Jacques Duclos arrived in Paris in a diplomatic car which had followed the triumphant march of the Wehrmacht into the city. He would try, unsuccessfully, to negotiate with German Ambassador Otto Abetz the legalisation of the Party and its press. The PCF gave priority to defending Stalin's Soviet Union and resisting French 'reactionaries', be these the SFIO or the Radical Party or the collaborationist regime newly established in Vichy. The clandestine *L'Humanité* of 18 March 1941 declared that the 'Paris Communards have been avenged by the party of Lenin and Stalin. They will also be avenged by the people of Paris and the whole of France. Long live the Paris Commune. Glory to its martyrs.' There were parallels between 1871 and 1941, wrote Maurice Thorez and Jacques Duclos, and 'the capitalists of today are the worthy heirs to the Versaillais':

Seventy years ago, the workers of Paris seized power: it was the grandiose epic of the Paris Commune. The workers of France salute, with their Communist Party, the indestructible memory of the heroes of the Commune whose emancipatory struggle they continue against capitalism. But if French pro-letarians find inspiration from the lessons given in 1871 by the Communards, if they wish to follow the glorious example given in 1917 by the Bolshevik party which, under the leadership of Lenin and Stalin, turned the great dream of the Communards into a living reality by establishing socialism on a sixth of the globe, on their side the capitalists are the worthy heirs of the Versaillais of 1871. Today, like seventy years ago, only one thing counts for the capitalists, and that is the defence of their interests and class privileges.

It was fear of the working class that had chased the capitalists of 1871 into the arms of Bismarck, and it was once more fear of the working class, fear of the people of France which, in 1940, pushed the French ruling classes to 'throw themselves into the arms of Hitler'. It was through their 'class spirit' that French capitalists, betraying the national interest, had led France to war and defeat. In 1940, the Italian and German leaders openly boasted of their participation in the Spanish Civil War to bring down the Republic and destroy the Popular Front, but 'they could not have succeeded without the help of Chamberlain and Blum'. Chamberlain and Daladier, who, 'right up until the last minute, thought they could turn Hitlerite Germany against the USSR', wanted above all to liquidate the Spanish Popular Front through the crushing of the Republic; it was then 'necessary to demolish the French Popular Front, with the complicity of Blum, Dumoulin and other traitors'. Duclos and Thorez revealed that on 1 July 1939, the 'sinister' Georges Bonnet had announced to Abetz's predecessor in Paris the forthcoming campaign of anti-Communist repression in France, and that Daladier had spoken to his entourage of a 'seven-year war', his aim being above all to destroy the PCF and force the French people under the 'darkest of dictator-ships'. The PCF leaders understood that the Blums, Gamelins and Pétains had all given their approval to this policy, which could not but lead France to a humiliating defeat.[6]

The issue of 25 May 1941 quoted Communard poet Eugène Pottier, evoked the traditional Montée au Mur to commemorate the Bloody Week, and denounced 'defeatists and traitors':

> In 1870–1871, the heads of the military betrayed France; they rolled up like lapdogs at Bismarck's feet and could only find the strength to drown the heroic Paris Commune in blood. Today, yet again, bribed military chiefs betray our *Patrie*. Pétain and Darlan, despised by the people and transformed into prison warders, are turning France into a Hitlerite colony. They are ready to shed French blood for the invader of our national soil. In France, the Communist party led the fight against the treaty of Versailles which oppressed the German people and we are sure that there exist forces in Germany which will rise up against the super-Versailles imposed on our country by the Third Reich. … Against this policy, the people of France are gradually organising the Front of the Resistance; the workers, in order to defend their salaries, are joining trade unions; the peasants feel the need to unite; everywhere the anger of the nation is rising against our oppressors and against the traitors in their pay.[7]

Here we observe a crucial shift in the discourse of the PCF: they no longer attack the socialist 'traitors', while the 'Hitlerites' are now described as an enemy. But they still attack the Western 'imperialists': 'Messrs Chamberlain and Daladier likewise told us that they were struggling for democracy when they were turning France into a vast penitentiary. We were the only ones to oppose the Daladier–Chamberlain war. There will be more of us to organise the Front of National Resistance against the war of Hitler–Darlan.'[8]

The same underground issue of *L'Humanité* spoke of the last Sunday in May, the traditional day of pilgrimage by the people of Paris to Père-Lachaise in honour of the heroes of the Commune. If France had still been free, rather than suffering from the 'dual oppression of the invader and his lackeys', it would have been in their hundreds of thousands that Parisian workers would have marched that Sunday, 25 May 1941, 'at the call of the Communist Party', past the Mur des Fédérés. Instead France, oppressed and humiliated, was deprived of all its rights: 'German and French plutocrats, the Krupps and the Schneiders, the Siemens and the Lehideux harbour the same hatred of the Paris Commune whose memory lives on in workers' hearts.'

However, the article continued, on the anniversary days of the Bloody Week, the women of Paris, heirs to the glorious women fighters of the Commune, did march to the Mur des Fédérés and lay flowers in memory. They brought their children and showed them this Wall in front of which our forefathers fell, crying *'Vive la Commune'*. In front of this Wall, the young generations had made a solemn vow to follow the example of the heroes of 1871. It was in different conditions that the people would made their sacred pilgrimage to Père-Lachaise, 'their fists clenched with anger as they think of our imprisoned, our deported, but also with hearts swollen with hope at the thought that nothing can prevent the heroic struggle of our great Communist Party for *the liberation and independence of France.*'

At the bottom of the page was a small article on life in the land of really existing Socialism: 'In 1941, wages are going to be increased by 6 per cent in the Soviet Union. In 1941, social and cultural spending will be up by 14.6 per cent in relation to 1940 ... This is how Soviet power cares about the labouring masses. In the USSR, it is well-being and abundance that reign; in France, as in the other capitalist countries, it is misery and oppression.'[9]

This ambiguous line, which did not yet call openly for armed resistance against the Nazi occupier, was also expressed in *La Vie Ouvrière*, the PCF organ in the Nord zone, which was under direct military rule and had just experienced a wave of Communist-inspired miners' strikes. In its special issue to mark 1 May 1941, the paper declared:

In 1871, to break the Commune, the Versaillais requested and were granted the support of Bismarck. In 1918, to crush the German revolution, the capitalists across the Rhine asked for and received the military support of the French imperialists. In 1941, to protect themselves from the people's anger, the French capitalists have recourse to the support of the Hitlerite armed forces. Shielded by their bayonets, they are imposing the most odious reactionary regime on the people of France. All freedoms are suppressed. The politicians of the bourgeoisie, the socialist and reformist leaders offer up the most repugnant spectacle you could imagine. Yesterday hysterical chauvinists, today they prostrate themselves at the victor's feet. They are trying to drag wounded France into another war. Some on the side of Germany, others on the side of England.

This delicate balancing act was further elaborated upon in another special issue of *La Vie Ouvrière* entitled 'Vive la Commune!' Under the headline 'The face of treason', the traitors of 1871 – 'Bazaine, Galliffet, Thiers, Fabre, etc' – were put back to back with those of 1941 – 'Darlan, Laval, de Brinon, Déat, Dumoulin, etc'. The editorialist declared:

> This year, Paris and France will have other reasons to celebrate the anniversary of the Commune. As in 1871, the country has been dragged into an imperialist war. As then it is suffering under the yoke of occupation. As in 1871, the 'elite' of the big bourgeoisie betrays, and treats with the invader through fear of the people ... To recover the freedom and independence of the entire country; to use all the resources of France for the satisfaction of its inhabitants' needs; to restrain the financial and industrial powers who are stuffing their faces after defeat, just as they got fat before and during the war; to place the people's destiny back into its own hands; that is what the French people want, and that is what the Paris Commune will inspire in them.

However, the French people did not express that desire 'through the excesses of a frenzied chauvinism like the one that was found up until June 1940 in the hysterical manifestations of the traitors of today. For them, the German people is not responsible for the barbaric acts of its imperialists. They know that, after all is said and done, the entente between peoples will be achieved against capitalism and the warmongers of all countries. The Commune had its first revenge in 1917, on a sixth of the globe. The time is coming when other successes, in other countries, will come to avenge our 30.000 dead.'[10]

But everything was about to change. On the solstice of 1941, Adolf Hitler launched Operation Barbarossa against his recent Bolshevik allies. The world, and Stalin's position, were going to be transformed: as Moscow was threatened, Soviet Russia called for armed struggle by all the Communist Parties of occupied Europe, wherever they may be. This new situation came as a relief for anti-fascists who had found the Molotov–Ribbentrop pact a bitter pill to swallow. It would not, however, make the last days of the Last Communard any easier.

5

Death of a Communard

A rather rose-tinted view has been given of Lejeune's last days in the Soviet Union. *France-URSS* wrote:

1941: the Nazis were approaching the gates of Moscow. Adrien Lejeune was evacuated to Novosibirsk. Out there in the glacial taiga, Adrien was looked after – even mollycoddled – by his Siberian friends. Despite the indescribable hardships of that period, everyone took care of the old Communard. The people of the taiga sent him fish. Peasants of the steppe brought bread, lumberjacks some wood for the stove. Every time, Adrien was moved to tears by these gestures of sympathy, and every time he passed on these vital presents to the closest hospital. The Party, the People's Aid of the USSR, the Komsomol, the Pioneers, the trade unions of Siberia all ensured that Lejeune lacked nothing, even visits, and hardly a week would go by without workers, peasants and young people coming to converse with the veteran of 1871.[1]

The reality was much more complex. Along with other revolutionary veterans, notably from the Spanish Civil War, Lejeune was first of all evacuated to Peredelkino, a village of datchas south-west of Moscow that was very popular with Russian intellectuals. Here he had as company Spanish Civil War leader Isidoro Acevedo, and a woman who spoke French, Adela Nikolova, with whom Lejeune had been living in an apartment in Gorky Street in Moscow. An ardent Bulgarian patriot, Nikolova had been condemned to death in her own country, and spent some years in exile in France before moving to the Soviet Union.

Revealingly, in Nikolova's dossier is a confidential report by Kalinitchev, an officer in the NKVD secret police. Adela Osipovna Nikolova was born in 1887 in the town of Székely, Hungary; she later became a citizen of Bulgaria. Despite her peasant background she went on to obtain a degree in foreign languages, becoming fluent in Bulgarian, French, Italian, Spanish and Russian. She was not a member of the Party. From 1925 to 1932 she had been imprisoned for revolutionary activity in Sofia. In 1934 she emigrated to Paris then, in April 1935, she came to the Soviet Union. In 1936–37 she worked as a teacher at the Second International Home for Children of the MOPR, in the village of Monino, near Moscow. In 1938 she was promoted to deputy director of the home. However, in 1941, 'on the orders of the Comintern', she became Lejeune's companion and carer. Another note by the NKVD gave a very positive opinion of Adela Nikolova:

In 1929, when the Communist Party decided to prepare the people for an armed insurrection, she joined the revolutionary movement and, risking her life in a period of White Terror, served the Party exceptionally by looking after communications and sheltering hunted revolutionaries, etc. Comrade Nikolova is known as a generous sympathiser with the Communist Party, a good socialist worker and a devoted citizen of the Soviet Union.[2]

But the welcome for these evacuated foreigners was very far from the ideal of Communist internationalism. On 14 July 1941, André Marty wrote to the Bulgarian chief of the Comintern, George Dimitrov, on the situation of Lejeune and of the international volunteers evacuated to Peredelkino hospital. He enclosed a letter from Nikolova which stressed that the situation had not changed. In the same little bedroom lived Lejeune, Nikolova and the nurse. They were considered by the director and doctor as 'prisoners'. To his knowledge, the direction of the MOPR had given no instructions on how to receive Lejeune.

As for the fifty wounded foreign volunteers and the twenty Spaniards at Peredelkino, they were hardly any better off. The attitude of the home's director towards them had been 'incomprehensible' since the day of the Nazi invasion. He had deprived them of all cultural or physical activity, under hollow pretexts such as 'it was not the moment' to learn Russian, or to learn Arabic (this concerned an Algerian comrade); and he had forbidden these disabled veterans from working. He had dissolved the circle of German comrades studying the history of the Bolshevik Party, declaring that he could not authorise meetings of more than two persons. He had revoked all permissions to go to Moscow, where some comrades were following courses. He had built no protection against air raids, contrary to wartime decrees. Having dismissed the deputy-director (who, admittedly, was in no way up to the task) he declared: 'We have to kick all of these people out of the home; and I distrust all these foreigners.' In Marty's view, even if the seventy comrades included four or five elements who were 'not very good', it was scandalous to treat some great disabled veterans of the International Brigades in this way; all the more so as they had sent Dimitrov a letter declaring they were giving up 80 per cent of their pensions to help the organisation of the national militia. If such a situation were not remedied, there would inevitably be 'some serious incidents'.

The letter he enclosed from Adela Nikolova gave a first-hand vision of the distressing treatment of these international volunteers on the outbreak of the Great Patriotic War:

I cannot remain silent about our arrival the day before yesterday. Our reception was rather difficult. From the very first minute I felt a very wounding atmosphere for us. To receive us like that is incomprehensible. We were greeted like beggars asking for charity, and this state of affairs continues. I hope, dear comrade, that the matter will be sorted out and that I will be able to organise our comrade's life properly. Our collective has been outraged by the administration's way of doing things. From my letter you will appreciate how angry I am.

It seems that Marty's personal intervention improved the living conditions of Lejeune and his foreign companions. In Moscow, PCF representative Suzanne Ledoux, in a letter to Marty dated 1 October, seemed quite optimistic about the situation of the Last Communard, although the question of his belongings continued to be a problem:

On 24 September I went to Kratovo with comrade Gasset. We saw comrade Lejeune and I must say I was so happy to see the vivacity of mind of our old comrade. I will be glad to visit him again. Comrade Lejeune has learned that you are in Moscow and he has a strong desire to see you, he wants to come to Moscow, see the exhibition, make some visits. To live at last, he said, which is something lovely to hear from a man who will soon be 94! He has had some small problems ... He had been sent to a sanatorium, and they kept his trunk ... for four months he has been asking for it back, but without success.

By 14 October, despite the onset of the season of rain and mud, the SS Das Reich Division had reached the Napoleonic battle-field of Borodino, only seventy miles west of Moscow. In the Soviet capital, rumours circulated that Stalin had been arrested in a Kremlin coup and that German parachutists had actually landed on Red Square. As the end appeared imminent, thousands of Muscovites stormed trains in stations. Drunkenness, looting and food riots broke out, reviving memories of the burning of Moscow in 1812. A state of siege was declared. Lejeune, Nikolova, Acevedo and other exiles were now evacuated to Novosibirsk in Siberia, 2,000 miles east. Eventually arriving on 25 October, they were met at the railway station by representatives of the MOPR. Lejeune, Nikolova and Acevedo moved into the first floor of the 'Dinamo' building.

In June 1967, a Soviet journalist, U. Kandeyev, cited a number of testimonies he had gathered on Lejeune's brief sojourn in Siberia for the Novosibirsk evening newspaper. According to Valentina Mikhailovna Stepanova, of the MOPR, 'Lejeune was exhausted by the long journey, but he was in a good mood. He was a tall, thin man, who despite his advanced age, stood up straight. He spoke in a calm and rather faint voice.' E. Mamro, a professor of history at the Makarenko Pedagogical Institute, also met Lejeune:

> I do not remember the precise date of our meeting, but I remember that it was in November 1941. We were a group of MOPR activists visiting Lejeune. The concierge took us up to the first floor where he lived. When we entered the bedroom, the veteran of the Commune was sitting in an armchair, his knees covered by a brown checked blanket. We greeted him and began to speak with him. I remember his words, when he said that Siberia was very far from his homeland, France, and that it was cold in Siberia, but that the affectionate hearts of the Siberians had warmed him up.

During this time, Acevedo continued to make public speeches on the civil war in Spain. But he fell ill, probably due to a lack of vitamins, and the MOPR was forced to search out some carrots to improve his diet. The MOPR also looked after Lejeune, bringing him newspapers: 'Adrien Lejeune was interested in the situation at the front and asked the interpreter to find news of France for him from the Soviet information bureau. He had realised that the fate not only of the Soviet Union, but of the entire world, was being decided at the gates of Moscow.'[3]

In one of his investigations into this Communard in Novosibirsk, another Siberian journalist, Alexander Kukhno, evoked in dramatic fashion Lejeune's attitude in those dark days of the war:

> Leaning on his walking stick, he stands by the hotel window, clad in a warm dressing gown and a fur jacket sewn by Adela herself, wearing a cap with a tassel which was also made by Adela. His face, pale as marble, is motionless. Only his big thick moustache is twitching slightly. Outside, there is bright, blinding snow. Along the Red Avenue, the Siberian Red Army Volunteer regiments march to war. Lejeune's dark-blue eyes are piercing with love and sadness. He has no doubts of victory: they will defeat the enemy, but how many of them will return home?[4]

According to Kukhno, as the young volunteers left westwards, Lejeune thought of the Commune's elderly military commander, Charles Delescluze, who had died on a barricade during the Bloody Week.

At the end of 1941, André Marty sent a telegram addressed to Lejeune at the Soviet Hotel, Novosibirsk:

ALL FRENCH COMRADES SENT OUR DEAR LEJEUNE WISHES FOR NINETEEN FORTYTWO STOP CERTAINTY THAT THANKS TO GIGANTIC BLOWS RUSSIAN ARMY AND SOVIET PEOPLE AND ALSO THANKS TO HEROIC STRUGGLE FRENCH PEOPLE AGAINST HITLER AND TRAITORS WILL RECEIVE YOU IN OUR PARIS STOP FOR EVERYONE STOP ANDRE

According to some accounts, Lejeune received on that very same day a message from members of the MOPR stationed in the remote region of Narym, sending him their best wishes for his health and for the victory of the Red Army over fascism, which had enslaved France and other European nations: 'We are certain, dear comrade Lejeune, that you shall live to see that happy day and return home to a liberated French nation, to the place where you raised the red flag of the Paris Commune.' Deeply moved by this letter, Lejeune apparently wrote a passionate appeal to the wounded Red Army soldiers in this hospital in Novosibirsk, an appeal published by the Siberian press:

> I am the last one of those who fought, seventy-two years ago, on the barricades of the Paris Commune, for the freedom of mankind. Then I was young and courageous like you and hated tyranny. Today my country is again under the Germano-Fascist yoke, but revolutionary traditions and the French people are not dead... And the time is not far away when the people will liberate itself from the Germano-Fascist occupiers. I am already too old, my dear friends, to visit you. But my desire is that you receive this letter for the New Year and wish you a prompt recovery. Long live the glorious Red Army! Long live the Paris Commune!

The dossier in the Comintern archives contains a photograph of comrade Lejeune taken in Novosibirsk, on 3 January 1942, a few days before his death. There is also this letter from Adela Nikolova to Marty:

Our dear comrade Lejeune is no more, he has died an innocent victim of this monstrous war unleashed by fascism. Our sad departure from Moscow, his acute bronchitis, the thousands of kilometres to cross, the Siberian climate, all contributed to the weakening of the heart and the body. Finally, he had a urological complication that his body could not overcome. On 9 January in the morning, he looked better, I washed him thoroughly, he was very happy, for he has taken great care of himself right to the end, he took his breakfast in the bed he rarely left, and said he felt better. I went out for a few minutes, and on returning he told me he was cold, the nurse told me she had already given him a hot-water bottle, that the patient was beginning to feel cold, I had him drink a little tea with a drop of wine, he drank, he coughed and suddenly he felt tired. I was in fact waiting for a medical visit, I telephoned the doctor to come without delay, at six his usual doctor, his urologist, and two professors arrived immediately. The consultation took place, a bloodletting, some injections to support the heart, and some leeches were ordered and applied by the sanitary personnel of the Polyclinic. One of the professors told me: comrade Lejeune is in a bad way, maybe we can save him; but given his advanced age, we must be prepared for anything. The patient calmed down a little. At around midnight the professors were still around him. And the professor who was holding his pulse told the nurse: 'Injection, quick!' The injection was given but death had already done its work. Our dear comrade stopped suffering, his last months were for this old man months of unbearable physical and moral suffering.

Adrien Lejeune had died 'surrounded by the affectionate and sincere care I gave him with all my heart. He died surrounded by the most attentive and cordial care of the doctors! He died surrounded by comrades of the MOPR, and the Party which sent a representative.' His remains were accompanied to the last resting place used by all the organisations of the city of Novosibirsk. Nikolova concluded:

> A fine revolutionary life has ended. The last fighter of the Paris Commune has closed by his death the list of those who fought in those glorious days for human liberation. Our dear comrade did not have the joy of seeing the final victory that is emerging so brilliantly and joyfully in the firmament. He did not have the joy of seeing his free Paris, the Paris he loved so much. In his last days he was aware of the brilliant victories won by our valiant Red Army over the army of Hitler. We will defeat them! Final victory is ours, it's starting already, he would tell me, and he was happy. Those were the last moments of our dear departed comrade Lejeune. I shouldered my duty to our comrade faithfully and lovingly right to his grave.

Isidoro Acevedo also wrote to his former comrade of the Spanish Civil War, expressing his deepest sorrow at the death of comrade Lejeune, as well as regrets at the old man's treatment:

> As you undoubtedly know, I had to use my status as a member of the Central Committee of the Spanish Communist Party. I asked, by letter, the Party secretary for the Novosibirsk region to intervene to cancel our journey to Tomsk. After a pleasant

exchange with this comrade and accompanied by comrade Nicolova, who was very conscious of the reponsibility for this delicate mission, everything was sorted out satisfactorily. If we had not taken this measure and had resigned ourselves to going to Tomsk, given the conditions in which Lejeune found himself, we would certainly have arrived there with his corpse.

In response to the death of the Last Communard, Marty wrote an article of homage, which was also translated into Russian, and a statement on behalf of the PCF Central Committee. He repeated common errors – birth in 1846 and emigration to the Soviet Union in 1928 – but also added a patriotic dimension that was in keeping with the terrible new times. On the eve of his death, Marty wrote, Lejeune declared: 'My one desire is to see the Hitlerite hordes crushed! And to see Paris and France free once more from villains and traitors!' For the third time in his life, he had experienced aggression by Germany against France. His heart 'bled at the thought that his Paris, which thanks to the indomitable courage of the Communards had avoided German occupation, was now sullied by the Hitlerite jackboot. He denounced the vile treachery of those who this time have succeeded in handing France over to the Germans.'

According to Marty, when on 15 May 1940 Lejeune learned that the Germans were at Sedan, he exclaimed: 'Sedan, so it's starting all over again? So they still have their Bazaines and MacMahons? Yes, if MacMahon holed up at Sedan, it was because he was afraid of us, because he was afraid of Paris, because he was afraid of answering to the people of France, much more than of the Prussians.' When Lejeune learned that the Germans had just entered Paris, he sat up in bed, despite his ninety-four years, and exclaimed: 'It can't be true.' He could not believe such treachery and dishonour were possible. As a great patriot, this made him suffer terribly, but, as he got weaker, he told the comrades who never left his bedside: 'Paris, I must see Paris freed from the brutes and bandits who are sullying it! To see Paris again, our beautiful Paris cleansed forever of fascists and traitors!'[5]

On 2 February 1942, from Ufa, in the southern Urals, Marty replied to the carer of the Last Communard, thanking her for the information on his last moments:

> You know full well how much we cared about him and how we hoped to bring him back to that Paris he loved so dearly and of which he had been a hero during the Commune. I am sure I express the feelings of all our Party and the workers of Paris in warmly thanking you for all that you did for him. We will not forget that it is thanks to your devoted care that his last year was much less hard for him to bear, despite the suffering imposed by this war. Be sure of our deep gratitude.

But there remained a few small things to ask of Nikolova:

> First of all, I want to know exactly where he is buried and how to recognise the place. Obviously, on the day of the liberation of France, we want to bring our father Lejeune back to Paris. Furthermore, I have been told that everything that could serve as a souvenir of him has been gathered at the agitation section of the Party committee. Could you tell me exactly what has been kept and in what condition these

objects have been wrapped, and their labels, so that we can receive them without a problem. I would be grateful if you could pass on to me the last interesting photographs concerning him so as to later put them in the archives of the French Party. We should also be glad to have your own photograph along with that of Lejeune.

Adela Nikolova replied on 19 March 1942:

Alas I was not able to accomplish the task I had given myself to hand back alive the last combatant of the Paris Commune to the workers of Paris. Death was stronger than me. Yesterday to commemorate the Paris Commune, I went to the cemetery with two French women to lay flowers on the grave of our dear comrade. I remembered that last year, we were already in our little apartment to receive the first visits on this occasion. In the evening we had some people around for dinner, and in a short speech he said: We are commemorating the seventieth anniversary of the Paris Commune, the old Communard is still with you, I want to live to see France free, my Paris in the hands of the workers but do not forget comrades that I am too old, who knows if I will have this honour. Yesterday, we had a soirée devoted to the Paris Commune and the MOPR. Comrade Acevedo said a few words. We observed a minute's silence to commemorate the memory of our dear comrade Lejeune and all those who have fallen gloriously for this grandiose and sublime cause.

On the subject of Lejeune's grave, Nikolova added, he was buried in the city cemetery. The Party had charged a special guardian to look after everything and the MOPR had asked an artist to make various sketches for the monument. Nikolova took this opportunity to give her own 'humble opinion' on this proposed monument:

> As the ashes are going to be transferred away from here, it is in my view pointless to make a big monument which would, given the war situation, take months to construct. A beautiful marble column with an inscription, and an artistic enclosure of wrought iron, could be quickly done and look quite elegant. I would like all this to be done while I am here. I will have the tomb photographed, and I will give you indications of the place so you have that to hand.

Nikolova assured Marty that she had handed over to the Party Committee all that comrade Lejeune possessed: his clothes, bedlinen, shoes, an album of the Commune and personal photos. There remained a few small objects in their apartment in Moscow, that in her haste she could not take. She would send her photo as soon as she could, but for the moment did not have one to hand: 'I have a mania about not being photographed, but for the circumstance I will do it happily, to be beside the photo of our old comrade.'

Marty replied from Ufa on 7 April 1942:

> I understand very well how much you have been touched by the loss of comrade Lejeune. At least you had the merit of softening the last months of his life and bringing him out of that isolation which he found so difficult. We too thought on 18 March of our fraternal soirées spent with father Lejeune,

when his so lucid, so Parisian mind was sparkling. I competely agree with your opinion concerning the grave. No grandiose monument but a simple column that enables us to remember where he is resting. It is of course understood that, as soon as circumstances permit, father Lejeune will be brought back to Paris. Please inform on my behalf the Party comrade responsible for this. Besides, in this period, all expenditure must be made for the war and that fits very much with our general attitude.

Concerning the rooms they shared in Moscow, he went on, comrade Germaine Fortin had been charged with checking that everything was still there. She had written to Marty immediately after Nicolova left, to say a woman had come and taken away a suitcase and various objects. She mentioned, for example, that the commemorative glass they had given to old father Lejeune on the last 18th of March was no longer there. In his post-scriptum, Marty transmitted his friendly regards to Acevedo and asked Nicolova to tell him that his letter had been passed on to Dolores Ibárruri, *La Pasionaria*, the female figurehead of the defeated Spanish Republic. Ever vigilant and suspicious, Marty finally asked for more details on the two French women who had gone with her to lay flowers on Lejeune's grave.

Nikolova also received a short letter from another PCF representative in Moscow, Raymond Guyot:

As you must have thought, we have been saddened by the loss of our dear father Lejeune. I often think back on the moments we spent together just a few days before we left Moscow and which, alas, were the last. Life is sometimes very sad. And some losses touch us deeply. He must have suffered a lot psychologically, he being so sensitive. At least you softened those last moments.

On 7 May 1942, Nikolova, still in Novosibirsk, wrote to Marty about the apartment in Moscow:

It seems that a female comrade of the Comintern now lives there. The manager of the home said that the person whom I charged with examining the state of the inventory has done the inventory. He also said that the charcoal portrait of our old comrade has been taken by the Comintern with his books, only the books are mine. He said that on the night of our departure, a woman entered our home and took a suitcase. In that tragic night of our departure, who could think of taking other people's possessions?

Ever diligent and reliable, Nikolova then filled him in on the two French women who had accompanied her to Lejeune's grave. One was Madeleine Kalashnikova, former regional secretary of the Friends of the USSR in Marseilles. She had been employed at the French section of Radio Moscow until 1935. She had been evacuated to Novosibirsk while her husband was at the front. The second was one Lorraine de Rémiémont, who had been in the country for thirty years. She had a child out of wedlock. To earn a living and bring up her child she had had to expatriate herself, being unable to find work in France 'because she had sinned'. 'How nice the laws in capitalist countries are!' exclaimed Nikolova. In short, she came to Russia as a primary school teacher, married and had 'three beautiful little boys'. She was a member of the Communist Youth. Nikolova concluded:

> In the coming days I want to go to the cemetery to see if they have started to make a few preparations concerning the grave. Spring has come, but it is still cold in our Siberia, it snows every other day. I have never seen such a climate, the weather changes at least ten times a day. At midday it is stiflingly hot, and in the evening, it snows, and you have to put your winter coat back on. This climate is very tiring. Comrade Acevedo is not so bad despite his rather frayed nerves, he has thinned and aged in a striking way. However, the conditions he lives in are very good, the food is sufficient and also good; who knows if we will have the happiness of getting out of here safe and sound.

Nikolova also replied to Raymond Guyot:

> I too often think of the pleasant moments we spent with our father Lejeune. He loved you dearly. It was a joy for him to see you. You are right to say that he suffered psychologically to find himself in Siberia, far from his friends, it was infinitely painful for him. He always would say: oh my friend where are you. I want to know before I die who sent me here. To calm him down I would tell him that comrade Marty asks every day by phone for his news, then he was content. Poor old man, if he had died in Moscow surrounded by all his friends it would have been his last joy. Ah, how many lives have been broken by this accursed war!

The Siberian Communists went out of their way to pay homage to this now deceased symbol. To prove this, the propaganda secretary of the regional committee in Novosibirsk sent a telegram to George Dimitrov, informing him that on Sunday 11 January the remains of comrade Lejeune had been displayed at the 'Agitation Point' of the city from ten a.m. to four p.m. Thousands of citizens had filed past the body of comrade Lejeune. The organisers of the Party, the Youth and the MOPR and other Soviet organisations had lain wreaths. The guard of honour was made up of militants of the Party, the Communist Youth, commanders and commissars of the Red Army, and delegations of Stakhanovites from the factories. The funeral procession drew thousands of people, and there were speeches from the regional secretary of the Party and the president of the regional committee of the MOPR. André Marty's tribute to Lejeune was read out at the meeting.

The inventory of Lejeune's possessions was finally passed on to Marty. Among the last surviving 'dear little personal things' of the Last Communard were: a telegram of congratulations to Lejeune for the New Year; a book of poetry in French; an envelope containing six photographs; an album, 'La Commune de Paris', containing fifty-eight photographs; a watch, spectacles in a case, a ruler, two knives, three manicure sets, a jumper, four sets of dentures, two lancets, 691 roubles in cash; a little glass ('a gift'); five pairs of socks; an autumn coat; a winter coat; two waistcoats; a summer hat; a winter hat; and a wooden walking stick.

On 11 January 1942, *Pravda* published a short article 'in memory of the veteran of the Paris Commune'. Significantly,

the Party daily chose to omit the sentences in Lejeune's declaration on the Commune which referred to its defeat: now was
the time to fight the descendants of the Prussian army.

During this period of the Second World War, the vision
of the Commune changed significantly among the French
Communists, who had now thrown themselves into the armed
struggle against the Occupation and its collaborators. In May
1942, the underground *L'Humanité* declared, with more than a
soupçon of 'frenzied chauvinism': 'French patriots, unite and
take action against the Boches and their lackeys, the traitors
Laval, Pétain and Darlan. Kick the occupiers out of France'.
If, on this seventy-first anniversary of the Commune, the
people of Paris could not march freely in front of the Mur des
Fédérés, flowers of memory would nevertheless be laid on this
sacred place. If they could not march, it was because Hitler
was afraid 'not only of the living but of the dead'.

On Sunday 31 May the Gestapo and the French police at
its orders would 'sully by their very presence' the necropolis of Père-Lachaise. However, the article continued, nothing
could prevent the patriots and revolutionaries of today from
honouring their ancestors of 1871. The best way to celebrate
the memory of those who died fighting was 'to fight'. Hitler
was afraid of the Communards who 'gave an imperishable
example of patriotic and revolutionary struggle'. For the
Nazis, there was nothing more fearsome than 'patriotic resistance to their oppression, to the traitors of Vichy, Pétain, Laval,
Darlan and Co.' The article's subheadings reinforced this new
image of the Commune: the Paris Commune was the revolt
of the People against the traitors; the people of Paris betrayed
and sold; Paris handed over to the Prussians; the Prussians

in Paris; Bismarck and Thiers united against the Commune; collaborators of yesterday and today.[6]

In February 1944, the year of the Liberation of Paris, the third clandestine issue of the Journal of the *Marraines* [female sponsors] of the 'Jean Jaurès' Detachment of Snipers and Partisans, published by the Union of French Women (National Front), announced that their journal's name was changing because the number of armed resisters was growing:

> From now on, we are no longer *marraines* of a detachment but of a company, the 'Paris Commune' company whose name recalls the courageous story of the Parisians sold to Thiers by the Germans in 1871 and who did not wish to submit. The Combatants of the Commune have been calumnied by those who were afraid of the patriotic sentiments of the people of France. But thanks to current events, all French people understand the burst of revolt and indignation of a people that did not want to live under occupation. The Laval of the time was Thiers, the sinister old man who drowned the revolt of the Parisians in blood. The Valiant Snipers have decided to pay homage to the Paris Commune to baptise a company that is fighting against the same enemies as in 1871.[7]

Thus, among French Communists of the interior, the Paris Commune regained a meaning that linked France and the USSR, communism and patriotism. But in the clandestine Communist press of the times, there was no mention of the Last Communard who had died in Siberia in the darkest days of the war.

6

The Return of Lejeune

In August 1944, Paris was liberated and the following year saw the first post-war *Montée au Mur*. The people of France could once again lay flowers on the graves of its heroes, and the French Communist Party, now the country's most popular party after its considerable sacrifices in the Resistance (75,000 members shot, it claimed, by the fascists), could put on an impressive show of strength. On 17 March 1945, at the Japy Gymnasium, near Père-Lachaise, to an audience of tens of thousands, the recently returned (and amnestied) leaders Maurice Thorez and Jacques Duclos celebrated the Communards as heroic and ardent champions of the national and republican cause. The crowd committed themselves to intensifying the war effort to crush fascism in Germany and elsewhere.

As a sign of renewed unity, the Communists and Socialists agreed to hold a joint demonstration at the Mur des Fédérés on 27 May, to commemorate the heroes of the Paris Commune, assassinated by the 'Pétains-Versaillais' of the time. *L'Humanité* reported a massive gathering at the Mur, led by the daughter of Zéphirin Camélinat, where the tirelessly repeated slogans

included: Death to Pétain! Punish the traitors! Purge now!
Better food! and Let the people speak! For seven hours, hundreds of thousands filed past the Wall, raising fists and casting
red carnations. There were 'countless' women, an 'ardent'
youth, representatives from the nearby Red Belt, and survivors
of the Nazi death camps. Portraits of Stalin were everywhere
and the crowd shouted: *Vive Thorez! Vive Marty! Mort à
Franco! Vive Tito!* Later, the novelist Hélène Parmelin evoked
the first post-war commemoration in these terms:

> Seventy-five years later, after a horrible night that lasted
> five years, the people of Paris were once more marching up
> towards the Mur des Fédérés, this time carrying the tribute of
> a victory, a power, an experience. 'This is why', said André
> Marty that same day, 'we are obliged to remember today that
> without the people, nothing is possible.' The people, assem-
> bled above so many ancient corpses, stood up at the dawn
> of time, singing in that May rain … At the gate to the cem-
> etery, a flock of Friends of the Commune were coming in,
> old, white- or grey-bearded men, surrounding the daughter
> of the Communard Camélinat, with the name of a shepherd-
> ess, Zélie.[1]

In *L'Humanité* and Parmelin's novel, there was no allusion
to Adrien Lejeune, but he was not completely forgotten. On
23 March 1945, André Marty paid homage to Lejeune at a
meeting of the Friends of the Commune. He told them that,
for the small colony of French communists in the USSR, he
had been 'an object of permanent veneration': every 18 March
they would prepare a fraternal meal for him. Marty recalled

how on 18 March 1940, during the *drôle de guerre* (phoney war), Lejeune had asked many questions about the situation in France, and 'to each name he gave we replied "arrested" or "deported".' Such was the case with the veteran communist trade unionist Pierre Semard, of whom Lejeune 'spoke all the time'. Semard would eventually be shot as a hostage by the Nazis. But Lejeune rejoiced in the fact that Thorez and Duclos had escaped the clutches of the Third Republic's 'henchmen' and 'traitors'.

On the morning of 16 June 1940, Marty had to tell him the terrible news that the Germans had taken Paris. Lejeune replied simply: 'It can't be true'. He then slumped in his armchair and exclaimed: 'Back in 1871 we had traitors like Trochu and that scumbag Thiers. But the Germans did not sully Paris, we were there with our bayonets.' Marty returned on the evening of 13 July to announce Pétain's 'coup'. This time, Lejeune did not move: 'When we gave up Paris, we lost everything.'[2]

Thus Marty presented to his overwhelmingly Communist French audience a rather selective version of the last days of the Last Communard: the compromises of the Nazi–Soviet Pact were forgotten, as were the hardships faced by Lejeune and other foreign comrades. The emphasis was on both French patriotism and attachment to the Soviet Union, the pillars of the PCF's identity at the end of the Second World War.

As for Adela Nikolova, the NKVD report tells us that after being, from 1941 to 1943, the carer of Isidoro Acevedo, 'on the orders of the Comintern', she took her retirement and resided in the Home for Children in Gorky Street, Moscow. Then, according to Jacqueline Jourdan, Adela Nikolova 'piously gathered together all the objects that belonged to Lejeune and, back in her liberated country, sent them to France to decorate the Museum for Living History in Montreuil'. Nikolova remembered:

> He always told me: 'My most ardent desire is to rest at the Mur des Fédérés, next to my fellow fighters who fell to give our country a better life.' I promised in front of his coffin that I would do all I could for his desire to be fulfilled, and I would like my French comrades to do whatever is necessary to permit the transfer of his remains to the country of his birth. I am sure that the Soviet Union will do this wholeheartedly.

While waiting for these wishes to come true, Adrien Lejeune's grave was always covered with flowers. According to Jourdan: 'When it is very cold, these flowers resemble drops of frozen blood, and when the blue sky extends over Siberia, they flourish like a flag symbolising the continuity of the barricades of the revolutionaries of Paris and Petrograd, Moscow and Novosibirsk.' As for Acevedo, he was president of the MOPR until his death in Moscow in 1952.

What explains the non-return to France of Lejeune's remains, and his temporary disappearance from the memory of the Commune? First of all, the great protector of the Last Communard, André Marty, was quickly discredited in the French version of the show trials that ravaged the newly established people's democracies. On 25 May 1952, Marty was accused of factional activity and links with the police. Marty was expelled from the Party and, after trying to group together some last supporters, including the very Trotskyists he had once persecuted in Spain, died in 1956.

With the loss of Marty, Lejeune lost a champion and a personal memory.

Secondly, the memory of the Commune was not a priority for the PCF in the two decades that followed the Liberation. References are rare in the Party archives. For example, on 19 March 1951, the Secretariat decided to 'cancel the meeting of 20 March for the commemoration of the Commune'.[3] Instead, its deliberations were dominated by the 'struggle for peace' and 'struggles for demands' – Korea, Vietnam and Spain. On 23 April 1951, it was not a question of commemorating the Bloody Week but of the anniversary of the execution of Resistance heroes Georges Politzer, Jacques Solomon and Jacques Decour. On 24 May 1961, the Secretariat discussed the Evian accords between the French government and the Algerian nationalists of the FLN and 'the victory of the forces for peace'.

For the first mention of Lejeune in post-war France, it was necessary to wait for a tiny article in *Le Monde* of 12 April 1956, entitled 'A Communard buried in Siberia'. In one of its recent issues the Soviet weekly *Ogonyok* had published a photograph of the grave of Lejeune, 'a French Communard who left France for the USSR in 1928'. The article in *Ogonyok* was written by a certain U. Medvikov. How, he asked, had the French Communard found himself in Novosibirsk in the winter of 1942? Medvikov offered the now conventional narrative: a young self-educated proletarian who volunteered to fight the Prussians, before fighting on the last barricade and miraculously escaping the firing squad; a French Communist of the first hour, who was welcomed by the USSR in 1928.[4] There followed his appeal to the Red Army, but shorn of any reference to Stalin, who had been denounced by Khrushchev in his 'secret speech' to the Twentieth Congress of the CPSU in February of that year.

Lejeune's credentials as the Last Communard could even be challenged. In 1960, the cultural review *Europe* published a brief but fascinating memoir, 'A child during the Commune', by one Alexis Truillot. Born in 1863, Truillot was still alive and well. His grandson, André Mathieu, presented him thus: 'In front of his television set, in a brand new block of flats in Marseilles, sits a man who has never ceased to be young, and writes poems as he waits to celebrate his hundredth birthday.' Born in Paris, the son of a radical-minded printer, whose old maidservant had witnessed the execution of Louis XVI in 1793, Truillot had an extremely precocious introduction to politics. During the Commune, he had met the journalist Jules Vallès and the poet Jean-Baptiste Clément. With his schoolmates, he was a member of the 'Vultures of Juarez' (named after a street in northern Paris) who served as couriers for the Communards. Truillot recalled watching the guillotine burn on the place Voltaire, helping to build barricades and, finally, helping Communards to escape bloody Versaillais repression.

After the Commune, Truillot became friends with the Symbolist poet Stéphane Mallarmé before moving to Algeria, where he worked as an archaeologist. He remained politically radical: as a member of the editorial committee of *La Revue socialiste*, he wrote articles criticising the colonial administration and corresponded with Friedrich Engels and Benito Mussolini, among others. However, it seems that in the twentieth century he had withdrawn from politics to concentrate on excavating Roman ruins, before returning across the

Mediterranean in the last years of French Algeria. His commemorative 'use' was therefore limited.[5]

Concerning the eclipse of Lejeune in France, Jean-Pierre Gast, a historian from Bagnolet, explained that Adrien Lejeune left for the Soviet Union 'in 1922 [*sic*]. He had no more contacts. Locally, it was ages since he left. There was no transmission of mcmory. The memory was re-established thanks to research done afterwards. There was a will to do a bit of research into his origins, which began from the 1960s onwards.'[6]

Indeed, the 1960s saw a revival of interest in the history of the Paris Commune, and a 'return' of Lejeune to public awareness, in France as well as in the USSR. Communist journalist Jacqueline Jourdan was a pioneer in this. To her work can be added that of another historian from Bagnolet, Michel Picard.[7] Their research finds an echo in that of Siberian journalist Alexander Kukhno, who took advantage of the relative liberalisation of the Brezhnev years to methodically follow the tracks of the Last Communard, among other neglected figures. On 18 March 1968, he published in Novosibirsk's evening newspaper a particularly interesting article, 'Two Portraits. Notes of a writer', which exhumed the memoirs of the avant-garde painter Kliment Redko, theoretician of 'electro-organism' and 'luminism'.

Research into material on the Last Communard took Kukhno to the Marx-Engels Library in Moscow. He learned from the library's director, Tamara Dmitrieva Belyakova, that there existed a portrait of Lejeune which had been displayed a few years previously at the Society of the Franco–Soviet Alliance, and then at the Library. Unfortunately, Tamara Dmitrieva could not remember the name of the artist and had mislaid the address of the portrait's owner. She continued to look for a few days, without success, but promised to keep Kukhno posted.

Nearly a year had passed when he received a letter in which she said: 'Recently I received a phone call from the wife of an artist called Redko, who did the portrait of Lejeune when he was alive. She has the portrait' – and gave him the woman's contact details. That very day the journalist spoke with the artist's wife, Tatyana Fedorovna Redko, and a few days later took the plane for Moscow. The last known portrait of Lejeune had to be displayed in Novosibirsk, the city where Lejeune lived and died, and where, apart from the monument on his grave, there was no material trace of his presence since all his belongings had been sent back to Paris in 1946.

In a cramped one-room apartment, its walls covered with pictures, an old woman recounted the story of her husband's life while showing his paintings one by one. Many were French landscapes executed in an impressionist style, amid a few 'very beautiful portraits of women – regular strokes, light colours: almost icons'.

Then Madame Redko opened a small box from which she lifted one painting after another. There were scenes of Central Asia, of the Moscow suburbs, of corridas in Spain, the Mediterranean coast, a Breton fisherman, Komsomol girls in Moscow, portraits of scientists and famous artists ... And then the portrait of Lejeune appeared: a grand old man seated with a walking stick among pine trees, dressed in a thick cherry-coloured peignoir. He did not look ninety-three years old, 'but rather a thousand. A striking contrast in colour showed up his puffy eyelids, emphasising the extreme age of the venerable

Portrait of Lejeune,
artist unknown (circa 1940)

Communard who had been crushed neither by serious illness, nor poverty, nor by awareness of imminent death.'

Kliment Redko had painted Lejeune at the sanatorium of Barvikha, near Moscow, between August and September 1940. Paris had just capitulated and France was occupied by the Nazis: there were more and more arrests and executions of Communists, many of them Lejeune's friends – all the leaders of the French Communist Party had been condemned *in absentia*. When Lejeune heard that Paris had fallen to the Germans, 'his physical pain diminished – he got out of his bed and declared that it could not be true.' He could not believe that the French would have capitulated to the Germans without a fight. It was in these painful circumstances that Redko painted his portrait. As Kukhno gazed at it, he read a desperate resolve in the old man's eyes, as if he was saying to himself, 'Be patient, Lejeune. Be patient. You must live to see the day of victory!'

Later, Tatyana Fedorovna and Kukhno went together to the Library. Everything was there: the memoirs and articles by Redko on Picasso, Cézanne and Seniak, the journals, the drawings, and an autobiography in three volumes. Kukhno read Redko's monograph published in Paris in 1929, with a preface by Lunacharsky. From 1926 to 1933, four exhibitions by the artist took place in France. Turning the pages of Redko's journal, he found that there was another name next to that of Lejeune: Isidoro Acevedo.

'So Kliment Nikolayevich made a portrait of Acevedo!' exclaimed the journalist. 'Yes, that's right,' said Tatyana Fedorovna. 'I have two of his portraits of him; but how did you know his name?' Kukhno explained how venerable a figure Acevedo was: Spanish writer and revolutionary, founder-member of the Spanish Communist party, member of the Central Committee, head of the Spanish International Organisation for Aid to Revolutionary Fighters, 'one of the Spanish nation!' 'Grandad' Acevedo, as he was affectionately called, had created clinics on the front line, before founding orphanages in Valencia and organising the evacuation of Spanish children to the Soviet Union.

In the summer of 1940, while he was on holiday in Monino, near Barvikha where Lejeune resided, Kliment Redko had done two portraits of Acevedo. He recorded in his journal:

23 August 1940. In two hours I am going to ask for authorisation to spend some time at Barvikha where I intend to make a portrait of the last of the French Communards, Lejeune,

who is ninety-three years old. I saw him two days ago and, to be frank, I left him with great sadness. Lejeune could be polite and attentive; but there was very little strength left in him. He showed me an album with scenes from the Paris Commune, and then, with the help of a nurse, he went out onto the terrace. Now I think of him: pale, holding a walking stick, he is sitting in a wicker chair, with some pine trees in the background.

On 24 September 1940, Redko described how, with the Soviet scientist and agronomist Leon Abovyan he had entered Lejeune's bedroom:

He was weak and ill on his bed. We stayed for a little time in his bedroom, exchanging words interrupted by long silences. I had already noticed a wide-rimmed straw hat belonging to the Last Communard when, suddenly, Lejeune asked the nurse to pass it over. Getting up from the bed, he put it on with his characteristic elegance. We laughed but our laughter was mixed with sadness. It was very difficult to make a portrait of Lejeune. You had to be very patient to achieve a lifelike painting. Finally I found the perfect moment to capture his likeness: he is sitting by the lake and admiring how the wind 'plays' with the water. The leaves of the trees are yellowing, it is autumn.

Kukhno ended by quoting the homage to Lejeune by Acevedo, published in *Soviet Siberia*:

Our comrade Lejeune is dead. I had met him for the first time many years ago, at the cemetery of Père-Lachaise in Paris, during one of the demonstrations which took place each year in front of the Mur des Fédérés. He was with Camélinat in 1932 [*sic*], and some six or seven veterans of the Revolution. Of this small group, only Lejeune was left. We cared very much about him, which he deserved as a relic of the World Revolution. But neither science, nor the attention given him by those who cared so much were enough to prolong the life of this man and, tragically, he has died. With him has vanished the last man of the great revolution which, for the first time, gave political power to the working class and prefigured the greatest revolution in human history – the October Revolution. Let us pay homage to him, but as true revolutionaries: in the present, struggling ferociously against fascism until its extinction, until the glorious day when the flag of the Paris Commune and the Great October Revolution will fly over the entire world.[8]

Thanks to Kukhno's investigative efforts, the portraits of Acevedo and Lejeune were now exhibited in the Art Gallery of Novosibirsk.

On 17 March 1968, in *Soviet Siberia*, Kukhno reported on his further investigation 'in the footsteps of Communard Lejeune', that began lyrically:

With a glove, the schoolgirl sweeps away snow on the grave of the Communard. Here, on this very Square of the Heroes of the Revolution, she has become a Pioneer and made her solemn oath. She wants to know more about the life and the struggle of the last participant in the Paris Commune. Who is he? Why is he buried beside the heroes of the civil war in Siberia?

There followed an account of Lejeune's youth based on the MOPR brochure of 1931. But the ever-curious Kukhno also cited a new source, notes published in Leningrad in 1937, where Lejeune described his betrayal and arrest in a more detailed and, most probably, untruthful manner:

On the morning of 28 May it was foggy. Seeing that there was no hope of victory, my comrades went home. Nevertheless, they did not feel safe in their homes – the concierges, under threat of arrest, were obliged to reveal the names of the Communards. As for me, I was not far from my parents in Bagnolet. But I knew that on my arrival in Bagnolet I would have been either caught by the rich peasants or killed by a gendarme. I was thinking of what to do when suddenly I thought that my godmother, a kind peasant woman, who did not live far away from the rue des Rigoles, could give me shelter. So I ran over there. I knocked on the door, but when she opened it, she refused to let me pass and so I was obliged to force my way in. At that point she started to shout at me: 'You stupid fool! You're going to have us all killed! Get out! Out! They're going to shoot us all!' Her cries attracted a patrol and I was surrounded. A corporal examined my hands and screamed at me. The commander of the patrol ordered: 'Put him with the others!' The others were a hundred men arrested like me, and at midday on 28 May the last cannon volley of the Commune could be heard in the distance. The Commune had been vanquished. The time of bloody repression had begun.

Kukhno still relied heavily on Lejeune's own telling of the story: escaping execution 'by accident', attacked by a crowd of bourgeois on the way to Versailles. The journalist cited the official record of his trial, but claimed inaccurately that he had indeed been betrayed by a 'gentle peasant woman'. Kukhno repeated the myth of the ingenious defence lawyer, but he got closer to the truth when he described Lejeune's imprisonment on a coastal hulk and his adherence to the socialist parties of Vaillant and Guesde. Kukhno concluded: 'All those who remember him describe him as a man of extraordinary charm and spiritual tenderness, qualities he retained to his last breath.'[9]

All in all, Kukhno was a passionate and perspicacious journalist who tried, within obvious limits, to shed light on the Lejeune affair. Another of his articles, 'When was Communard Lejeune born?' went further than his French counterparts in the quest for the truth, taking to task a new tourist guide to Novosibirsk which asserted that Lejeune had been born in 1846. Yet Lejeune himself had declared that he was born in the village of Bagnolet in 1847. Had the old Communard simply forgotten his date of birth? After all, the anonymous author of the guide was not the only one to say 1846, the date indeed engraved on his tombstone. But Kukhno returned to the available documents. There was a 'Foreigner's Residence Permit', which gave the date of birth figuring on his passport: 1847. There was also a birth certificate, kept in the *mairie* of Bagnolet. One hundred and twenty-one years ago, a French functionary had written, on headed notepaper, 'with a clerk's very careful handwriting', not only the year, but also the month, the day and even the time of the birth of Adrien Lejeune.

Kukhno asked his readers: 'Where is the problem if we add

one or two years to his life: what is the point of criticising this in public?' But 'we have to, because one error can be followed by many others'. Not long before, an article by Kukhno as submitted to *Literaturnaya Gazeta* asserted that Lejeune had come to the USSR in 1930. The Siberian journalist bought the published newspaper and read: 'had already come in 1928'. Had the proofers changed the date after consulting the guide? Yet it was obvious that neither the author nor the editor of the guide had checked the original documents, instead recopying erroneous information found in another book. The results of such 'studies' were dubious, to say the least. 'You want to study Lejeune?' an archivist had asked Kukhno. 'But there have already been so many publications, and radio and television programmes, about him.' Kukhno had looked up everything previously written on Lejeune, and found there 'information, but with no reference to documents'. With more than a hint of exasperation, he concluded:

> I have doubts about all that has been written on Lejeune in the last twenty-five years and, consequently, I go and consult the archives and museums. I seek out people who knew Lejeune personally, I spend months and years on it, I put up with the compassionate smiles of friends and the sceptical laughter of old truth-hunters. We must remember Lejeune, not only the anniversary of the Paris Commune, and therefore it is imperative that he be studied in a detailed and accurate fashion.

For Kukhno, it quickly became clear that the sole source of all the errors found in texts on Lejeune was the obituary by André Marty, published on 11 January 1942. But, he cautioned, one could not be too hard on Marty as it had to be remembered that, in January 1942, the Central Committee of the PCF had gone underground, while the executive committee of the Comintern and the central committee of the MOPR were evacuating to different cities. It seemed that Marty did not have Lejeune's personal file to hand, and the obituary had to be written in haste. Kukhno therefore consulted Lejeune's residence permit and above all the summary of the trial in 1872 to establish the facts on his sentence. The journalist challenged the myth, propagated in the Soviet press, notably *Komsomolskaya Pravda*, of his deportation to New Caledonia:

In his 'Memoirs', Lejeune writes about his life on a floating prison in Port d'Auray and in the fortresses of Belle-Île and Port-Louis. I cannot find these names on a map of New Caledonia. These names cannot be found in French Guyana either, but I see them on the French coast. It seems that an author has manipulated terms like 'forced labour' and 'old convict', with all the consequences we know. It is difficult to believe that Lejeune would have been silent about forced labour, and life on a floating prison was hardly more pleasant than exile. Maybe he was judged and sentenced again? Everything is possible, but no document supports this version of events. No one has studied in detail the biography of Lejeune between 1877 and 1930, the year he came to the USSR. The study of the life of the Last Communard must be accomplished in a methodical manner. The repetition of out-of-date information and poetic beauties only postpones the solution to this complex and important task. The search for materials on Lejeune continues.[10]

Unfortunately, Kukhno himself does not seem to have pursued the investigation much further. The files in the Marxism–Leninism Institute, in Moscow, and the Historical Service of the Ministry of Defence, in Vincennes, remained unopened.

Nevertheless, in Novosibirsk and Bagnolet, the Last Communard seemed to be gradually emerging from oblivion. The municipality of Bagnolet decided to name a street after their lost son. On New Year's Day 1969, the local bulletin announced that a new street had been created as part of the major rebuilding of the Moulin district of the town, only a few hundred metres up the rue Sadi-Carnot from the house where Lejeune was born. It was decided to name it after this local incarnation of the Paris Commune and the Bolshevik Revolution. If the bulletin correctly gave Lejeune's date of birth, his father's profession and the address where he was born, the Last Communard was described erroneously as having been deported to New Caledonia until 1880. He was also wrongly described as a close companion of Edouard Vaillant, leader of the United Socialist Party, though Lejeune's membership of this precursor of the PCF is probable (if not verifiable). Finally, the inhabitants of Bagnolet were told that at the age of seventy-nine, in 1926, he left France for the Soviet Union and stayed in Moscow where he could at last see fulfilled around him his Communard dreams. It was in Novosibirsk that death would take him, after a life entirely devoted to the revolutionary struggle.

But the figure of Lejeune took on even greater symbolic importance with the commemoration of the centenary of the Paris Commune. This centenary came in an extremely tense political context, especially on the left. It is no surprise that in the course of the 1960s, the Paris Commune became of interest to French radicals seeking alternative models to the failed bureaucratic regimes of 'really existing socialism' and recently 'liberated' Third World countries. In *The Proclamation of the Commune* (1965), Henri Lefebvre, one of the PCF's foremost philosophers until he left the Party in the late 1950s, declared that the Paris Commune was the greatest *fête* of the nineteenth century. A spontaneous and volcanic effervescence, it blew away the sediment of State, bureaucracy and dead culture. During that brief springtime, the Paris proletariat redefined labour, consumption and urban space itself: the Commune was the precursor of a 'revolution of everyday life' that had nothing to do with Stalinist authoritarianism.

Inevitably and typically, Lefebvre was denounced as a plagiarist by Guy Debord and the Situationist International. Nevertheless, both looked to the Paris Commune as inspiration for a more authentic form of communist revolution. For the Situationists, the Commune anticipated a new form of society that would be 'realised art'. The Communards had no leaders and the fact that they all played around with weapons was a way of 'playing with power'. What's more, they practised a 'revolutionary urbanism', attacking on the ground the petrified signs of the dominant organisation of daily life, recognising social space in political terms, refusing to accept that a monument such as the column on the place Vendôme – a symbol of Napoleonic militarism – could be neutral or innocent.[11]

The collective memory of the Commune would be reactivated as never before by the events of May '68. The historian Danielle Tartakowsky remarks: 'The Commune departed the necropolis. It rediscovered the streets.'[12] If the main reference for the workers who joined the general strike was the Popular Front of 1936, the Paris Commune was vividly present in the discourse of the students. Although the contexts were very different, it was not difficult to see similarities between the opening of 'red clubs' in churches during the Commune, and the staging of intense intellectual debates in places like the Odéon theatre, Sciences-Po, the Beaux-Arts, the Sorbonne and, above all, in the street. On 11 May, the morning after the Night of the Barricades, the graffiti scrawled on the walls of the Latin Quarter included 'Long live the Commune of 10 May' and 'There are 3,000 communes in France … we're now at our second!'

On the walls of the capital, in the left-wing and far-left press, and in songs, the memory of the struggles of 1871 were always present. As during the Commune, an ephemeral press was born. Among these journals, *L'Enragé* would run for only thirteen issues, distributed by student action committees. The very first issue contained the words to *L'Internationale* along with another poem by Eugène Pottier, 'Assassin!', denouncing the police brutality against demonstrators at the Mur des Fédérés on 24 May 1885. In *Les Lettres françaises*, edited by Communist poet Louis Aragon, an article by Bruno Marcenac, 'Show Me Your Hands', related the experience of a young female student at the hands of the CRS riot police: 'Black hands accused, judged and condemned. Like in another springtime, that of the Commune, when the hands of the rebels were black with powder.' In *Le Nouvel Observateur*, student leader Daniel Cohn-Bendit celebrated 'our Commune of 10 May'. There was a veritable outpouring of hatred for Adolphe Thiers: students at the lycée Thiers in Marseille demanded that their school be renamed the lycée de la Commune de Paris, while militants desecrated the huge Thiers mausoleum at Père-Lachaise.

Three years after the events of May–June 1968, the French Communist Party was seeking a Union of the Left with the Socialist Party: a broad alliance was needed, bringing all progressive social layers together, in order to peacefully overcome 'state monopoly capitalism'. At the same time the hegemony of the PCF was being violently challenged by *gauchiste* groupings, who accused the party and its allies in the CGT trade union of having betrayed the revolutionary hopes of May '68. To this could be added growing anti-Sovietism and anti-communism, especially after the Warsaw Pact's crushing of the Prague Spring in August 1968 and the 'normalisation' of Czechoslovakia that followed. The PCF had to assert itself as the legitimate heir to those who had, in Marx's words, 'stormed the heavens'.

Roland Leroy, a member of the PCF Politburo and responsible for relations with the intellectuals, played a key role in the commemoration of the Paris Commune. Among his personal papers at the archives of the PCF is a dossier devoted to the 100th anniversary.[13] At the meeting of the Secretariat of 19 March 1970, Leroy set out the case for a National Committee for commemorating the centenary. It was essential that this National Committee, including the celebrities, be 'dominated by communists', but it would organise a 'People's Assembly' in Paris on 18 March 1971, then, on 23 May, there would be a mass march to Père-Lachaise cemetery.

Leroy then presented to the Secretariat a planned appeal from the Committee. Based on national democratic traditions, the Paris Commune tended towards a socialist transformation of society in one of the greatest capitalist countries of the time. It destroyed the former state order and replaced it with a new type of democracy, demonstrating that social progress posed the problem of the handover of power from one class to another. National in origin, it was 'profoundly internationalist'. Its very failure served as a lesson to its successors. It was by drawing on the Commune's experience that Lenin and the Bolsheviks, building on the teachings of Marx, were able to successfully lead the revolution of October 1917 and defeat the Whites and the foreign interventionists – whereas the Commune had been beaten by the Versaillais who benefitted from Bismarck's help. The appeal concluded:

> The French working class and the people of France will commemorate the hundredth anniversary of the Paris Commune. They will honour the memory and the sacrifice of the first harbingers of a new society. In the face of attempts to disfigure it, they will assert the deep meaning of the Parisian revolution of 18 March 1871. They will also express, one century after the Commune and half a century after the Soviet revolution, the depth of socialist aspirations in contemporary France.

On 16 June 1970, a note by Leroy spelled out what was at stake politically in the commemoration of the centenary of the Commune: 'The importance of the centenary derives both from the event itself and its insertion in the overall political situation. The various ideological currents and political forces situate themselves in relation to them. It will be the occasion for a "lively ideological struggle".' Hence the need to clarify the chief themes on which the PCF should focus, and the best way to approach them: avoid an exclusively commemorative point of view, and link the centenary to the Party's current perspectives; take into account the political situation and the ideological struggle that the commemoration would give place to.

According to the Communist leader, these themes would be: the Commune as 'a new *type of State*', a new and higher form of democracy 'founded upon the real and fecund participation of the masses'; the necessity and role of the party of the working class; and the national and international character of the Commune. It was therefore necessary, Leroy continued, to envisage these themes in the light of the reality of the Commune, its contribution to Marxism and the ulterior theoretical and political developments, and, in this way, to 'struggle against attempts to denature the Commune – from the right or the left – and oppose it to the experience of the movement. To struggle therefore against bourgeois, reformist and *gauchiste* interpretations.' Leroy finally addressed 'various questions', one of which was the need to 'ask the Soviet comrades for the return of the body of Adrien Lejeune'.

The decisions of the Politburo in the months leading up to this commemoration offer insights into the climate and stakes of the time. On 14 January 1971, the Politburo noted:

The developing anti-Soviet campaign is fundamentally caused by the accentuation of class struggle on the international and national scale. Against this background, the bourgeoisie is using everything that is happening in the Soviet Union and other socialist countries: the events in Poland; the trial in

Leningrad; questions relating to the Jews in the Soviet Union. In France, this anti-Soviet and anti-communist campaign is aiming to distort and sow doubts about socialism; the bourgeoisie is trying to use our correct positions, which express certain differences with the USSR, to lend credence to the idea that the PCF is distancing itself from the USSR.

On 4 March 1971, the Politburo stressed that communists had to be 'vigilant concerning provocations by *gauchiste* and fascist groups'.[14] The PCF leadership's other preoccupation was rapprochement with the socialists. That same day, Georges Marchais wrote to Alain Savary, secretary of the Socialist Party: 'As we have already informed you, we think that the Centenary of the Paris Commune should be celebrated in common with all democratic forces. ... We also seek an agreement in principle on the organisation of a united demonstration at the Mur des Fédérés at the end of May.'[15]

In Moscow, the commemoration of the Commune provided an opportunity to reassert the close ties between the Soviet and French Communist Parties; relations between the two parties had been in crisis since August 1968, when the PCF condemned the Warsaw Pact intervention in Czechoslovakia (the only time the party ever opposed a Soviet military intervention).

In *L'Humanité* of 18 March 1971, its special correspondent in Moscow, Max Léon, reported on the centenary celebrations of the Commune in the capital: a solemn assembly attended by numerous Soviet leaders including Leonid Brezhnev, general secretary of the CPSU, Boris Ponomarev, long-time head of the party's international department, and Mikhail Suslov, the unofficial chief ideologue. The PCF was represented by

Guy Besse, member of the Politburo, and Henri Rol-Tanguy, architect of the Parisian insurrection of August 1944 and member of the Central Committee. Ponomarev 'was very pleased with the ties of fraternal friendship that had long united the two Communist Parties, a friendship based on the principles of Marxism–Leninism and proletarian internationalism'. The Soviet communists, the workers of our country, he said, 'greatly appreciated the fact that the PCF had always acted as a faithful friend of the USSR and our Leninist Communist Party'.

Hailing the profound changes that had taken place in the world to the advantage of socialism and progress, the speaker praised the strength of the communist movement, which at that time numbered 50 million militants in eighty-nine parties. The Commune had been confronted with the problems of peace and war. Today, the communist movement was also confronted with this, but on a completely different scale. United, the forces of socialism, the international working class, and peoples' liberation movements could constitute an insurmountable obstacle to the warmongers. In the capitalist countries, the communist parties, taking inspiration from the Commune, led the revolutionary struggle by fighting 'opportunism' on both right and left, knowing that successes 'are only definitively achieved by the establishment of a new regime'.

In response and on behalf of the French Communist Party, Guy Besse saluted the CPSU and the Soviet people, stressing the deep solidarity between the two parties and peoples, the Soviet and French communist militants who were 'children of the Commune and children of Lenin'. Besse reminded the audience that the fights for democracy and for socialism were inseparable. Then he praised the profoundly national character of the Commune's struggle against the invader and against the Versaillais from whom they had wrested the tricolour flag; and also, its internationalist spirit. Heirs to the Communards, the French communists intertwined 'the defence of national interests and faithfulness to proletarian internationalism'. That was why, Besse declared in his conclusion, they combatted all forms of anti-Sovietism and stressed the 'eminent role played by the Soviet Union against imperialism, particularly in South-East Asia and the Near East'.[16]

Quite obviously, this declaration by Besse on 'anti-Sovietism', and his paean to Moscow's foreign policy, targeted Mao's China as well as the capitalist West. In February 1967, the proclamation of a 'Shanghai Commune' had been a major episode in the Cultural Revolution that rocked the People's Republic. Modelled on the 'bright flower' of 1871, for its twenty-day duration this Commune replaced the old bureaucratic administration with a people's government that excluded practically all of the former leading Party cadres and city officials.[17] Now, to mark the centenary, the Chinese leadership declared:

> At the time when the proletariat and the revolutionary people of the world are marking the grand centenary of the Paris Commune, the Soviet revisionist renegade clique is putting on an act, talking glibly about 'loyalty to the principles of the Commune' and making itself up as the successor to the Paris Commune. It has no sense of shame at all. What right have the Soviet revisionist renegades to talk about the Paris Commune?[18]

In the eyes of a small but noisy band of Maoists in France, China represented creative, revolutionary Marxism versus retrograde statism – although it is evident that the Maoist view was still dominated by the tutelary figure of the party.

On 19 March 1971, *Soviet Siberia* published an anonymous article entitled 'A Parisian in Novosibirsk', telling readers that the name of Adrien Lejeune was 'chiselled into the red stone placed next to the common grave of the heroes of the Civil War who were brutally tortured by [Admiral] Kolchak's soldiers'. The text reproduced the version of events found in the MOPR brochure of 1931, and, if generally accurate, did not include the modest but significant recent discoveries by Kukhno. What's more, it even claimed that, after his release, he was banned from Paris and 'sent to an isolated and distant village'.[19] The piece was accompanied by the obligatory quotations from Marx, Engels and Lenin on the history, the success, the failure and the meaning of the Paris Commune.

In March 1971, *Etudes soviétiques*, the glossy magazine published by Moscow for an increasingly less receptive French market, tried to give a glowing image of the land where Lejeune had died. Articles outlined the Five-Year Plan in the countryside, commended the scope of major public works and the expression of a 'Soviet humanism' in the social security system, and portrayed Novosibirsk as 'a city of dynamic young people'. Then there was the urgent question of the Paris Commune and its contemporary meaning: its heritage was 'now, and in its entirety, the property of the international proletariat, of its communist and workers' parties active on every continent'.[20] The illustrations included an image of the flag of the Commune's 67th Battalion gifted to the workers of Moscow in July 1924, as well as photographs of two Russian female Communards, Elisabeth Dmitrieff and Anna Korvin-Krukovskaya.

Of more interest was an article by the literary critic Yuri Danilin on his encounter, in the early 1930s, with the second-to-last Communard in the USSR, Gustave Hinard, as part of his research into the poetry of the Commune. Unfortunately, the poet Achille Le Roy had already died in 1929. Danilin managed to get an interview with Adrien Lejeune, only to find that

> he could tell me nothing about [his] favourite songs, neither the old ones nor the new ones born in 1871, nor about the Communard poets who remained mysteries to me, such as Vémar, Isch-Wall, and Guérin … It even seemed to me that due to the passage of time, Lejeune had forgotten quite a lot of things. Then I learned that he had been a pharmacist in his working life, and so far away from literary circles. On taking my leave, I reproached myself for having bombarded with silly questions this ancient man who sent me a guilty smile.'[21]

In July 1934, Danilin finally tracked down Gustave Hinard, in a Moscow rest home: 'A stooped old man in a grey suit. A walking stick in his hand, he is constantly lighting his pipe for a puff. Hands with swollen veins, reddish and shrivelled skin. The hand he stretches out to me is so light, so weak, so immaterial, that I scarcely dare to shake it.'[22] But he remained a 'man of the people' and began to recount the last days of the Commune, his relations with Maxime Lisbonne, and the atrocious death of Eugène Varlin, as well as his own fate. The ending is by now familiar: 'Downcast, shaking his head, he grows withdrawn and his words become confused. It is not, in general, easy to hear him, but you would not dare ask him to repeat himself. Thus the end of the story remained unclear to me.'[23] Only at one moment did he suddenly become animated: 'The Communards did not burn Paris! The Communards did not destroy museums! They were honest people! I did not burn a thing!'[24]

The article concluded with an evocation of Lejeune's last resting-place:

> By night his grave lies solitary among the evergreens of the Square of the Heroes of the Revolution. In the daytime, there are always people here. In summer, they bring flowers from the fields; in autumn, crimson maple leaves; in winter, branches of Siberian oak with dried leaves. And sometimes, even when it is very cold, on the marble turned silver by frost, you can see roses and scarlet carnations. They resemble drops of blood, the drops of blood that fell on the ground in front of the Mur des Fédérés at Père-Lachaise.[25]

Back in 1971 France, the Communist policy of alliance with the socialist left seemed to be bearing fruit. At the municipal elections, the left made significant gains. On 22 March, the Politburo noted that 'the results in Paris are among the most significant on the political level.'[26] The following day, the PCF held a triumphant meeting on the Commune at the Mutualité. In his speech, Roland Leroy described the Paris Commune as 'a beacon that nothing can ever mask again', and inscribed it in the current Party line. According to Leroy, 'the Commune was the first revolution which had for its goal the establishment of socialism, even if the idea many Communards had of socialism was vague and utopian.' Leroy emphasised the decisive role of the International, and explained how the Paris Commune succeeded in 'making the Republic a reality': through its militants and elected officials, through the separation of Church and State, and through free and compulsory education. Leroy insisted upon the large number of politically active workers in the Commune, which was 'the State as emanation of the working people'. Its social achievements were not insignificant: cancellation of unpaid rents, limitation of the working day, workers' cooperatives and crèches for women. One lesson could be drawn from the failure of the Commune: the peasants had to be mobilised. Which allowed Leroy to make a link with the political situation in France:

> Our Party considers it indispensable to unite all the anti-monopolist social layers for an advanced democracy and socialism, all the anti-monopolist layers, that is to say around the working class, both urban and rural. ... This celebration is not for us a ritual ceremony, it is also a profound homage, made of willpower, initiative and audacity so that workers and democrats can build together, in France, a Commune for our time.

Other speakers followed at the Mutualité. The future PCF general secretary, Georges Marchais, declared to the audience that 'socialism is the future'. A. M. Rumiantsev, of the Central Committee of the CPSU, described the October Revolution as 'heir to the Commune'. Miklos Ovari, secretary of the

Central Committee of the Hungarian Socialist Workers' Party reminded them of Leó Frankel. Arturo Colombi, a leader of the Italian Communist Party, spoke of the echoes of the Commune among Italian workers. Albert Norden, of the Politburo of the GDR's Socialist Unity Party, praised 'the first German socialist state faithful to the teachings of the Commune'. And Stefan Olszowski, member of the Politburo of the Polish United Workers' Party, paid homage to the exploits of the Commune's Polish generals, Wróblewski and Dombrowski.[27]

Preparations continued for the return of Adrien Lejeune. On 8 April 1971, Jacqueline Chonavel, PCF deputy for Seine-Saint-Denis and mayor of Bagnolet, who had just been re-elected with an overwhelming majority, wrote to the president of the Novosibirsk Soviet, sending the municipality's warmest greetings:

> Having come to the Soviet Union in 1924 [*sic*], after suffering the extreme repression of the Versaillais, our fellow citizen found help and comfort amongst the Soviet people. The years he spent in your country and notably in Novosibirsk, despite the ordeals of the Second World War, lit up the end of his glorious existence. Measuring the character and the importance of the Great October Revolution, he wrote on this subject: 'I have seen the dream of the Paris proletariat fulfilled here.'

Although drowned in blood, the Paris Commune continued to 'exert its historical attraction upon the peoples struggling for their liberty. On the 100th anniversary of the Paris Commune, we thank you for fervently keeping alive the memory of our fellow citizen.' At Bagnolet's public library, in the avenue

Gambetta, there opened an exhibition on the Commune, while the cultural centre offered a show, 'Singing the Commune', led by legendary *chanteur* Mouloudji. The town's inhabitants were urged to view some of the Last Communard's personal possessions, now on display at the Museum of Living History in nearby Montreuil: a glass engraved with Adrien Lejeune's initials, and a watch he wore during the Commune and from which he 'never wanted to be separated'.

Unfortunately, the difficulties encountered by the PCF during the attempt at rapprochement with Guy Mollet's Socialist Party emerged clearly in the centenary commemoration. On 28 April 1971, Roland Leroy wrote to Jacques Enock, president of the National Committee for the commemoration: 'All the conversations we had showed that the leadership of the Socialist Party wanted to refuse our repeated proposals for a unity demonstration at the Mur des Fédérés. We sincerely regret this.'[28] The leadership also had to deal with the threat from the left of the Party. On 30 March 1971, the Politburo had decided to 'keep an eye on actions by the authorities and on the violence and excesses of the *gauchistes* which exasperate the great mass of the French people, including those who are unhappy with the current government, and allow the authorities to consider having a referendum-plebiscite on problems of order and public safety.'[29] This vigilant attitude was justified by the desecration of Communist graves at Père-Lachaise, including that of the 'Son of the People' himself, Maurice Thorez. On 4 May 1971, the Secretariat decided:

The demonstrations by *gauchiste* groups show that these continue to influence a fraction of the youth, notably the intellectual youth. We must not give up trying to win many young people over to correct positions. We must intensify the political struggle against the *gauchistes*. We must give very great importance to preparing the demonstration at the Mur des Fédérés.[30]

On 5 May 1971, Gaston Plissonnier addressed a letter to the Central Committee of the CPSU:

As was agreed, and for which we thank you, the ashes of Adrien Lejeune, the last veteran of the Commune, who died in the Soviet Union in 1942, are going to be transferred to Paris. We intend to organise the burial of Adrien Lejeune's ashes at the cemetery of Père-Lachaise in front of the Mur des Fédérés on 23 May 1971 on the occasion of the march for the centenary of the Bloody Week. We would greatly appreciate it if you sent a delegation appointed by the CPSU central committee, and we hope you will accept this invitation.

In a post-scriptum, Plissonnier informed the Soviets that following the instructions given by Maurice Schumann, the minister of foreign affairs, the French embassy in Moscow would have to provide 'a health certificate and an authorisation for the transfer of the body'. It went without saying that the administrative formalities 'would be more easily overcome if the remains of Adrien Lejeune were incinerated'.[31]

So things were falling into place for the return of the last Communard. But it is not known for sure if this symbolic gesture was the initiative of the French or the Soviets. The note written by Leroy in 1970 and the letter by Plissonnier quoted above seem to indicate that Lejeune's return was requested by Paris. But in conversation with this author, Jacqueline Chonavel asserted the contrary: 'Personally, I heard about Adrien Lejeune for the first time when his ashes returned to Bagnolet. We had not known before that Adrien Lejeune had lived in Bagnolet, that he was this Communard, one of the last, who lived in Moscow. It was then that we found out that Adrien Lejeune had lived in Bagnolet and that the Soviets wanted his ashes to be buried in Bagnolet. When we heard all this about Lejeune, we were completely flabbergasted.'[32] This version of events, which seems slightly curious given that a street had been named after Lejeune two years previously, was confirmed by Bagnolet's deputy mayor at the time, Daniel Mongeau:

> On the occasion of the centenary of the Paris Commune, the CPSU decided to keep the flag draped behind the body of Lenin, the flag was not going to move, but it also decided to show its friendship for the French people that had stormed the heavens, and the French Communist Party, by returning the ashes of the Last Communard. But what were we going to do with the ashes? Well, the first idea was that when they arrived at the airport, they would be brought back here, to Bagnolet. Then there was a whole discussion and it was decided to put his grave in the Party section facing the Mur des Fédérés.[33]

Meanwhile, various demonstrations were taking place at the Mur des Fédérés, all seeking to appropriate the Commune, against the backdrop of frequent violent confrontations with the police and even a bomb attack on the Thiers mausoleum. In the pages of *Rouge*, Alain Krivine's Revolutionary Communist League (LCR) presented thus its common demonstration with Trotskyist rivals Lutte Ouvrière (LO): 'It is the best possible riposte to the hysterical campaign by the PCF. Let no one be misled: the exploitation of the police provocation at Père-Lachaise is nothing other than a panicked reaction by the Stalinist bureaucrats in the face of the enormous success of the revolutionary demonstration on 1 May.'[34] Indeed, on 16 May, the LCR and LO managed to mobilise around 20,000 people. This *montée trotskyste* took place in an extremely tense atmosphere. *L'Humanité* condemned it as an 'anti-working-class demonstration'. However, Lutte Ouvrière congratulated itself on this success, which, it believed, would be just the start of better things:

> The international demonstration, organised by the LCR and Lutte Ouvrière and essentially bringing together the European sections of the Fourth International (Unified Secretariat), to celebrate the Centenary of the Paris Commune, has been an undeniable success. ... The entire demonstration, well organised, showed an extremely dynamic face. Red flags, banners, slogans, all loudly asserted the vitality of the Trotskyist movement in France and Europe. Even if the Trotskyist revolutionaries have not yet completely won over the working class, this demonstration proves that they have won over the youth. It remains to agree on aims to turn these promises into certainties on the road to the reconstruction of the Fourth International.[35]

Constant references were made to wildcat strikes at the Renault factories of Billancourt, Flins and Le Mans which pitted the 'Stalinist' CGT against *gauchiste* activists. *Le Prolétaire*, organ of the International Communist Party (Communist Programme), denounced 'the false communists of today who are the first to hide the true meaning of the Commune. The Commune was internationalism and revolution, but they see only patriotism and democracy; it was the dictatorship of the proletariat, but they deduce from that the need for an alliance with the middle classes.'[36]

Elsewhere on the far left, the anarchists of *Le Monde libertaire* republished works by Mikhail Bakunin and Prince Kropotkin to show the anti-authoritarian and even pacifist 'truth' of the Commune. The magazine remarked ironically that 'the men and women of the Commune are going to be converted into Marxist–Leninists, without forgetting Louise Michel, who successively approved of the Moscow trials, de-Stalinisation, Prague and the murder of Polish workers by progressive tanks.'[37] And the commemorations had not been the exclusive preserve of the Marxist or anarchist left: on 25 April, 3,000 freemasons of the Grand Orient of France had paraded before the Mur des Fédérés, resplendent in their aprons and insignia.

On 19 May 1971, Plissonnier wrote to Leroy: 'The Soviet embassy informs us of the arrival of Adrien Lejeune's ashes on Friday 24 May, on flight 251 from Moscow.' At a ceremony in Novosibirsk, a guard of honour escorted the coffin containing the remains of the Last Communard. The first secretary of the city's Party committee, Alexander Filatov, proclaimed to the crowd that Adrien Lejeune had remained faithful to

A guard of honour surrounds Lejeune's
exhumed coffin (Novosibirsk 1971)

the emancipatory ideas of 1871. The coffin left the Square
of the Heroes of the Revolution in order to be incinerated.
A Tupolev 114 would fly the ashes of the Bagnoletais Adrien
Lejeune home from Moscow.

The funeral urn containing these ashes was firstly displayed
in the hallway of the *mairie* of Bagnolet, where a large crowd
came to pay its respects. In the morning of 22 May, an official
Soviet delegation and one from the PCF central committee,
including the veteran leader Jacques Duclos, also came to pay
homage to Adrien Lejeune. The urn posed some unexpected
problems for the communist leaders of the Last Communard's
home town. According to Daniel Mongeau:

It was Jacqueline Chonavel who received the urn. Duclos arrived with the urn, because he was the one who had gone to fetch it at the airport. The urn arrived and all this came to Bagnolet. There was a catafalque. We organised a guard of honour, with some young communists, some old ones, some veterans, in the tradition of the workers' movement. So the urn arrived and Jacques Duclos passed it on to me, as secretary of the party and just recently elected deputy mayor. Well, I took the urn and I was surprised by its weight. But, thankfully, I didn't drop it.

Chonavel recalls likewise: 'Lejeune was cremated in the Soviet Union. And the urn came from over there. Because over there they have very heavy urns. Ours are lighter and we weren't expecting it. Oops!!' The transfer of ashes from one country to another could only be made in a lead container. Hence the weight. But there was a whole symbolism at the time. It was the CPSU, and this handover of the ashes was part of the symbolism. Several of those present had to stifle their giggles, because when it was her turn to hold it Jacqueline was not expecting it to be so heavy either. Mongeau added, with a rueful laugh: 'There was a whole team from the Soviet embassy. Well, they were very discreet, they were there for the protocol in the name of their country and their Party. They let the French get on with it. Of course, I'm not saying they were glad to get rid of that urn!'

That day, a demonstration at Père-Lachaise brought together two fractious marches: jostling with one another were the CFDT, the PSU, Force Ouvrière, the Socialist Party, the Alliance for Youth, the Socialist Zionist Group, Témoignage

Chrétien, Maoists and anarchists … although the Garibaldians were absent, in protest against the use of their name on a poster attacking the PCF.

The following day the big march to the Mur des Fédérés took place, convoked by the Friends of the Commune, the PCF, the Convention of Republican Institutions, and the CGT. There were 80,000 demonstrators, according to *L'Humanité*; more than 50,000, for *Le Monde*. On the front page of the Communist daily, Laurent Salini described the march in ecstatic terms.

There were 80,000 of us for the *Montée au Mur*. Never has so much been spoken and written about the Commune, as for this anniversary. And never has reaction done so much to obscure its meaning. The long cortège which, all through that Sunday afternoon, saluted the Mur des Fédérés bore witness to the fact that the Commune is at the heart of our struggles and this is because it was above all a workers' insurrection, a revolution for socialism, the first proletarian state. … Today, no progress is possible without the support, the participation of the workers, whose demonstrations express that hope. Today, nothing can be done without the working class and the working class can do nothing without its allies. But we are stronger. How the power of socialism has grown in one century!

Inside the Communist Party newspaper, Nelly Feld wrote a more expansive description:

Paris came up last on the march. It was six o'clock when the last group entered the main gate of Père-Lachaise. They still had to cross the cemetery to reach the Wall where a simple plaque reminds us of the Fédérés. In advance, wreaths of red flowers had been laid there. On a small coffin draped in red stood the urn with the ashes of Adrien Lejeune. By its side was his portrait. Many men and women held a red carnation. They threw it down as they passed. They threw it as if to bow down to salute the memory of all the combatants, at the spot where the Versaillais, shooting the last Fédérés, believed they had killed the Commune and stopped History, when it had only just begun.[38]

On the front page of *Pravda*, V. Sedykh wrote:

The immense crowd was in a great hurry, filling the districts of the French capital which spread from the place de la République to Père-Lachaise cemetery. For several hours, dense columns of demonstrators marched along the springtime boulevards as far as the Mur des Fédérés where exactly one hundred years ago, the tyrannical government of Versailles shot the rebel proletarians.[39]

The Parisians were there en masse, he went on, to pay homage to the Last Communard, who had left for the USSR in 1926 [*sic*]. Also in attendance were Georges Marchais, Jacques Duclos, Roland Leroy and many other leaders of the French Communist Party, as well as representatives of other democratic organisations and a delegation of the CPSU.

The march to the Wall could be seen as a great coup, a show of strength by the Communist Party and a riposte to the anti-Sovietism in the air. However, *Combat* noted that it was the memory of the drama of the Bloody Week that dominated: 'the

A scene from the march to Père-Lachaise with a banner
celebrating 'The Last of the Communards' (Paris 1971)

solemnity, the silence of this grave and slow crowd suggested
more a funereal homage to the dead of the previous century
than the hopes of their descendants'. The demonstrators filed
past the Wall and a stand where the Soviet ambassador and
leaders of the French left were seated. *L'Humanité* would evoke
the death of 40,000 Fédérés but did not publish any historical
article, preferring to place a political emphasis on the unity
that had to be recaptured in the present. No doubt this was the
reason for the proliferation of tricolour flags in the cortège,
which were not to everybody's taste.[40] Danielle Tartakowsky,
historian of Père-Lachaise cemetery and of popular demonstrations, placed this ceremony back in the context of other
Montées au Mur:

The communists felt threatened by the new avatar of the Commune that 1968 claimed to embody. They appealed to their original memory and reinforced their domination of the space *intra-muros* by proceeding to repatriate the remains of Adrien Lejeune, the last of the Communards, who died in Moscow [*sic*] in 1942. His ashes were buried opposite the Wall, beside Communist intellectuals and leaders. It was, for the first and last time, a reactivation of the Commune's meaning by a return to the origins.[41]

In *Rouge*, the Trotskyists of Krivine's Revolutionary Communist League sneered at this PCF attempt to hold on to the Commune. They boasted of the success of the LCR-LO joint march (a turnout of 50,000 according to them), comparing it with the 'pitiful' gathering organised by the reformist CFDT trade union on 22 May. As for the PCF's effort at recuperation of Communard revolt:

With the burial of the ashes of the Last Communard, it was the Commune that the PCF buried deep. It had the wherewithal for that since tricolour flags, the colours of the murderers, were widely dominant. The demonstration as a whole singularly lacked dynamism and enthusiasm. Even numerically, the PCF had not mobilised great crowds. If the cortège was long, it was also loose and very spaced out. Behind the Renault banner walked scarcely more than fifty workers. The ranks of l'UNEF-Renouveau [Communist student organisation] were particularly thin (a thousand at most). The Stalinists, desperate to show off their mass organisations, did not hesitate to disguise a few hundred already bearded Young Communists as 'Pioneers of France', an organisation for the under-twelves. A few sections of Young Communists chanted daring slogans: 'The Commune is not dead, let's continue the fight', 'Vietnam, Laos, Cambodia, the same fight'. But without finding any echo. On the pavements, old working-class militants were indignant to see the flag of the Versaillais in front of the Mur des Fédérés. Four demonstrations have marked the centenary of the Commune. Only one was a demonstration of communist militants, only one through its slogans, its enthusiasm and its size was worthy of the combat of the Communards. It was carried out under the flag of our Fourth International.[42]

The right-wing daily *Le Figaro*, which had been banned by the Paris Commune and had denigrated it ever since, also played down the Communists' success: 'On the level of numbers, the PCF and its allies undoubtedly scored some points off those who had demonstrated before them. Behind the Central Committee, the majority of people were young. And yet there was little spontaneity, and the procession was singularly lacking in ardour.'[43] The journalist reported that a few anarchists had tried to join the march and been promptly expelled by stewards. In the interests of 'balance', *Le Figaro* also quoted the archbishop of Paris, Monseigneur Marty, who opined: 'Rioting is perhaps merely the desperate expression of a dialogue of the deaf.'

In a September 2005 conversation, Danielle Tartakowsky returned to the meaning of the big Communist march on 23 May 1971, which she attended as a PCF student. While she did not share her party's contemptuous view of the Trotskyists, she inclined to think that the Last Communard had never really escaped oblivion:

> The Mur des Fédérés became a place of memory for the workers' movement and especially the PCF. Between the wars, there had been huge demonstrations, especially in 1936, on the eve of the electoral victory of the Popular Front. In 1968, 1969 and 1970, there were no demonstrations, but in 1971 it was the centenary of the Commune and all the organisations of the left decided to commemorate it. The far left, the socialists and the communists were struggling for supremacy. These organisations each mobilised to have the biggest possible demonstration and the PCF did not want the far left to win, which is why they decided to have Adrien Lejeune buried there in order to mix together the memory of the Paris Commune, the Soviet Union – which was under a lot of pressure at the time – and the PCF. It was the biggest march in the history of the Mur des Fédérés. I remember that this demonstration was important because I was a young student in the PCF and we were fighting the far left. But I don't remember a word being said about Adrien Lejeune.[44]

7

End of the Commune

For some, the Montée au Mur of 23 May 1971 was not without consequences. For example, Daniel Mongeau played down the idea of a fight to the death with the Maoists and Trotskyists, and rather emphasised the PCF's key role in the Union of the Left:

There was no competition with anyone at the time, because it was the Communist Party that dominated the left. And the context was one where the forces of money, the government and the media, all of them, were cultivating the theme of crisis, the crisis caused by the oil price shock. And the PCF ran a counter-campaign which argued that the crisis was not unavoidable, and that you had to fight with the PCF and for French production. Plus the fact that municipal elections had just taken place in March 1971, showing progress by the PCF, and this would be repeated in 1977. So it was a time when the PCF seemed to have the wind in its sails. We mobilised people around the idea of the Common Programme. We did this at demonstrations, and that was the biggest demonstration of all. … We didn't want to crush the *gauchiste* fly with a sledge-hammer, even if this fly could be irritating.

The early 1970s did see the ebb tide of the far left, even if the 1972 funeral of the Maoist Pierre Overney, shot dead by a factory guard, allowed his party Gauche prolétarienne to mount a massive show of support in the capital (a phenomenon the non-Communist left attempted to repeat in 1979 at the funeral of Pierre Goldman, who was buried to the beat of Caribbean drums). But the decade would also see the PCF overtaken in the polls by its social-democratic *frère-ennemi*, now led by François Mitterrand. In post-Mao China, the last vestiges of the Shanghai Commune had been dismantled by 1979, as Deng Xiaoping steered the country on a radically new economic course.

The break-up of the Union of the Left, and the crisis it provoked in relations between the Party and its intellectuals, led to the collapse of the PCF's Paris Federation and the electoral marginalisation of the party, even in the 'Communard' bastion of the 20th arrondissement. There would follow the communist calvary of the 1980s, the fall of the Berlin Wall and dissolution of the Eastern Bloc, and finally the humiliating scores for National Secretary Robert Hue at the presidential elections of 2002 (3 per cent), and for his successor Marie-George Buffet in 2007 (2 per cent) – well behind their old Trotskyist rivals.

As for Père-Lachaise and the Mur des Fédérés, their role as 'realms of memory' diminished. After 1975, the funerals of Communist leaders ceased to attract great crowds. It was rather the funeral processions of Jean-Paul Sartre and Yves Montand that got the far left back onto the streets. The wishes of the family seemed to prevail over party-political ones: in 1997, Georges Marchais would be buried in Champigny-sur-Marne, the town he had inhabited and represented in parliament. A year previously, François Mitterrand had made the last request that 'Le Temps des cerises' be sung, but this took place on the place de la Bastille, and was performed by an American.

The Wall became a national heritage site in 1980, and the annual commemoration is chiefly kept alive by the Friends of the Commune. The cemetery has not become completely devoid of political passion: in April 1988, Dulcie September, the South African leader assassinated in Paris by an apartheid regime death squad, was cremated at Père-Lachaise at a well-attended ceremony organised by the ANC, SWAPO and the PCF.

Nevertheless, the rapid decline of French communism has taken its toll on the memory of the Paris Commune to which it claimed to be the rightful heir. Jacqueline Chonavel, retired from national and municipal politics but still fiercely communist, told me:

I remember, but I was just a small kid at the time, when we all wore red stars at the sports club. It was a working-class thing, and the sports clubs and the youth movements were highly mobilised to commemorate the Mur des Fédérés, and I even remember there were choral groups, and poetry recitals, a whole sort of ceremonial and a very combative, very warm atmosphere. You felt that the Paris Commune really meant something to committed young people. ... What's left of it now? The name of a street [Adrien Lejeune].

This was echoed by Daniel Mongeau, who had succeeded Chonavel as mayor: 'In Bagnolet, though less than elsewhere, it's gradually being lost, it's turning into ancient history. Take a young secondary schoolkid today, and ask him about the Paris Commune. What would he say? That some guys from the suburbs robbed nuns and then the Sacré-Cœur was built. To expiate the crimes of the Commune.'

From a highly qualified stance within the Maoist tradition, Alain Badiou mourns the fading memory of the Paris Commune. In *The Communist Hypothesis*, he writes:

> Does the working class have a heart? Today, in any case, little is remembered, and badly so. The Paris Commune was recently removed from French history syllabuses, in which, however, it had barely occupied a place. The public offices are swollen with the direct descendants of the Versaillais, those for whom communism is a criminal utopia, the worker an outdated Marxist invention, the revolution a bloody orgy, and the idea of a non-parliamentary politics a despotic sacrilege.[1]

Nevertheless, for Badiou, the martyrdom of the Commune challenges us to think about politics 'outside of its subjection to the state and outside of the framework of parties or of the Party'.[2]

A similar assessment has been made by Kristin Ross, for whom, after 1989, the Commune was 'untethered from Lenin's apocryphal dance in the snow'.[3] No longer moored to the once dominant historiographies of official state communism and national French republicanism, the Commune can be viewed as a form of federated, decentralised community, organising its social life according to principles of association and cooperation. The seventy-two days of 'communal luxury' anticipated the encampments and occupations that burst spectacularly onto the world political scene in 2011.

The Paris Commune therefore remains a reference for some on the left, and the Mur des Fédérés is still a realm of memory. In September 2005, near to the Mur, I hid behind a hedge with the self-styled 'necrosopher' Bertrand Beyern (at that time, guided tours of the cemetery were strictly forbidden by the *mairie* of Paris). He whispered:

The cemetery is a place of illusion, a theatre where the dead seem to be with us, seem to sleep. Here, they 'rest' ... Here we see that the cult of the dead is the only thing believers and non-believers have in common. Here communist memory is inscribed in stone, granite and bronze. In the month of May, this corner of the cemetery takes on a peculiar hue, for 130 years on, people continue to commemorate the Commune. There are political demonstrations. Societies like the Friends of the Commune keep the tradition alive. Often I see real cherries on the grave of Jean-Baptiste Clément. And these days you often see Chinese delegations. Any Chinese person who comes to Paris knows the name, knows about the famous Wall. They ask me: 'The Wall! The Wall!' and they come here to pay homage because even if their country is evolving in the direction we know, they were still raised in the cult of the Communards. In a few square metres we have in condensed form the memory of the workers' movement and the whole turbulent history of the twentieth century. It is the only place in this cemetery where there are no flights of fancy. We are accustomed to seeing tombs that stand out for their humour, but here we find something more powerful, something more profound.[4]

That same day I crossed Paris to talk to Marcel Cerf, then ninety-five years old – grand-nephew of the Communard Maxime Vuillaume, biographer of the 'D'Artagnan of the Commune', Maxime Lisbonne, and doyen of the Friends of the Commune. Cerf confessed to me that, although he had been passionately interested in the Commune early on and had followed the huge funeral procession of Zéphirin Camélinat in 1932, he had only heard of Adrien Lejeune after the war, and especially at the time of the centenary. As neither a communist nor an anti-communist, Cerf offered this judgement on the Last Communard:

Obviously, we can't deny that Adrien Lejeune fought for the Commune, but we would have to see in precisely what conditions. During the siege, he was a member of the National Guard and even obtained the rank of sergeant, but after the armistice with the Prussians he surrendered his weapons. And when the Commune was proclaimed, he had no desire to resume a military role in the National Guard, and managed to find a job in the food supply service at the *mairie* of the 20th arrondissement. That meant he could avoid being in the National Guard. So he did this work during the entire Commune, until the start of the Bloody Week. And at the start of the Bloody Week he thought it would be preferable to get out of Paris. He was arrested at the gates of Paris by the National Guard and taken to the prison of La Petite

Roquette, where it was proposed to him to take back his role in the National Guard, because if he stayed in prison he would most certainly be considered a traitor. He therefore decided it would be better to get back into uniform, and it seems he fought bravely either at the rue du Faubourg St-Antoine, or the rue Ramponneau, as he himself said [*sic*]. In any case, he fought to the last day and was arrested on 28 May. ... As a combatant he was not perhaps absolutely exemplary, but he did fight for the Commune and for this reason deserves our homage.[5]

This is a nuanced judgement based on a precise knowledge of certain documents, which other evidence from Moscow and elsewhere can serve to complement. Adrien Lejeune was not the heroic Communard of Communist hagiography, but a man who played a modest yet fateful role in an event whose brief existence would come to haunt the left, and ultimately determine the rest of Lejeune's days.

The Bagnolet of today is very different from that of 1971, let alone 1871. In 2014, the last Communist mayor, Marc Everbecq, was defeated by the socialist *frère-ennemi*: Bagnoletais municipal communism therefore had a shorter lifespan than Adrien Lejeune. Given the crushing dominance of the left in this suburban town, there are no plans yet to rechristen streets: the rue Lénine is still adjacent to the rue Karl Marx; the College of Labour, Red Bagnolet's first ambitious project, still carries a bas-relief of a worker and a peasant brandishing hammer and sickle respectively. The very modest rue Adrien Lejeune is also there, extending beneath a block of flats occupied on the ground floor by a geriatrician's office, and opening onto neat

1960s-style *pavillons*, much sought after by the poorer 'bohemian bourgeois' who are being driven out of Paris by booming house prices. But the Grand'Rue, where Lejeune walked to and from the Commune, is in a sorry state: many shops are boarded up and covered with graffiti, though the house where he was born is occupied by a thriving couscous restaurant, Les Folies Berbères. The *mairie* that Lejeune and Roussel descended upon is dwarfed by the Mercuriale twin towers and a huge new town hall. The *périphérique* now prevents you from reaching Paris on foot. The city walls, of course, are no more. Instead, at the end of the Grand'Rue is the Paris International Coach Station, where Eurolines transport migrant workers from all over former Communist Eastern Europe.

At the end of this tortuous journey through the life and legend of Lejeune, it only remains to salute the Last Communard's entrance into fiction. In 1994, the Swiss novelist Jeanlouis Cornuz published *Les Désastres de la guerre*. At the start of this narrative we find ourselves in the rue Oberkampf during the last battles of the Commune, with 'Adrien Lejeune', his sweetheart 'Aline', and 'Arthur de Charleville', all three of them aged seventeen. Adrien fires the last shot of the Commune, after Aline has expired in his arms. Arthur will leave to pursue the brief but brilliant poetic career we are all familiar with. Adrien rediscovers his sister in Frankfurt, joins the Socialist International, gets to know Clara Zetkin and Rosa Luxemburg, takes part in the German Revolution of 1918, becomes the father of a son who will join the International Brigades, then ends up reaching the USSR, where he dies in 1942. In the sequel, *Les Caprices*, Cornuz writes:

Adrien Lejeune died during the war. After all the uncertain years he had lived through, forced to take such and such from his youthful idols, such and such from his old comrades, for so many traitors – not to mention the Nazi–Soviet Pact, which was not easy to swallow – he had had the double joy of seeing the USSR stand up to Hitler's Germany and, after the catastrophes of the first months of the war, see it recover, block the way of the invaders in front of Leningrad and Moscow, so much so that the hope of final victory became reasonable. His last years were lonely, for he had lost his wife at the start of the Spanish Civil War. He managed to feel glad about that, since it meant she had not seen the triumph of Franco. Lonely? And yet he was not alone, surrounded by younger men and women who had been born during the First World War and took him to be a sort of monument to Revolution – hadn't he experienced the struggles of the Commune, in 1871, then the German Revolution – or the bid for one – in 1918? He followed on the radio the deadly fight waged by the Soviet armies for the USSR and for the freedom of the people, the final struggle which would lead at last – you could hope – to the socialist and communist society evoked by Babeuf, whose fitting first name was Noel, one hundred and forty years before.[6]

Cornuz thus turns Lejeune into a container of history, an extra in a fresco of what he calls the 'cataract' of time. As a form of conclusion, I would say that this text leaves a lot to be desired: it creates arbitrary and implausible links between Lejeune and his times. His picaresque character as grand old revolutionary, betrayed by others and virtuous to the end, does not touch the reader.

The novel leaves out the elements that make Adrien Lejeune so interesting: his real and imagined life, with its convictions, friendships, moments of cowardice, half-truths, lies, shady corners and banalities, a story of property and theft at every level; the manipulation of memory and the (largely consensual) instrumentalisation of an individual who became a 'relic' of a cause; the randomness, the pathos and the cruelty of History. It seems that, much more than any novel, the documents and testimonies, swarming with contradictions and silences, constitute in themselves a historical drama and answer at least a few of the questions that a little black marble grave had raised in my mind on the morning of 10 November 1989.

Notes

Introduction

1 Fernand Chatel, 'Le dernier communard', *L'Humanité*, 22 May 1971.

1 Birth of a Communard

1 René Duchet, 'Le dernier des communards mort à 95 ans à Novosibirsk', *France-URSS* 37 (May 1971): 28.
2 The personal file of Adrien Lejeune, no. 517/1/192, is kept at the Russian Centre for the Conservation and Study of Historical Documents (RGASPI), Moscow. His autobiography (quoted) is in file no. 495/270/4985, at the same location.
3 Jacqueline Lalouette, *La libre pensée en France, 1848–1940* (Paris: Albin Michel, 2001).

2 Lejeune, Communard

1 Quoted in Jean-Pierre Gast, *Bagnolet, 1862–1935. Un beau jour le présent s'appelle l'avenir* (Paris: Messidor, 1988), pp. 19–20.
2 Ibid., p. 22.
3 Jacques Duclos, *La Commune de Paris à l'assaut du ciel* (Paris: Editions Sociales, 1971), p. 288.
4 Jacqueline Jourdan, 'Le dernier communard', *La Vie Ouvrière*, 24 April 1967, pp. 21–3.
5 *Bulletin des Amis de la Commune de Paris* 32 (Autumn–Winter 2007): 12–13.
6 *Journal officiel de la République française*, 13 May 1871, p. 984.
7 Service Historique de la Défense: 8/J/414.
8 National Archives, Paris: BB 24/761.
9 Cited in Jean Baronnet and Jean Chalou, *Communards en Nouvelle-Calédonie. Histoire de la déportation* (Paris: Mercure de France, 1987), p. 84.
10 Jacques Rougerie, *Le Procès des communards* (Paris: Julliard, 1978), p. 64.
11 Cited in Jean Maitron, ed., *Dictionnaire biographique du mouvement ouvrier*, vol. 9 (Paris: Editions ouvrières, 1971), p. 236.
12 Rougerie, *Le Procès des communards*, p. 87.

3 After the Commune

1 Duchet, 'Le dernier des communards', p. 29.
2 Charles Chincholle, *Les Survivants de la Commune* (Paris: L. Boulanger, 1885), p. 1.
3 Maitron, *Dictionnaire biographique*, vol. 9, p. 51.
4 See Madeleine Rebérioux, 'Le mur des Fédérés. Rouge, "sang craché"', in Pierre Nora, ed., *Les Lieux de mémoire*, vol. 1 (Paris: Gallimard, 1984), pp. 619–49.

5 Danielle Tartakowsky, *Nous irons chanter sur vos tombes. Le Père-Lachaise, XIXe–XXe siècles* (Paris: Aubier, 1999), p. 63.

6 Marx and Engels, *Writings on the Paris Commune*, edited by Hal Draper (New York: Monthly Review Press, 1971), p. 69.

7 Ibid., p. 73.

8 Ibid., p. 80.

9 Ibid., p. 83.

10 Ibid., p. 84.

11 Ibid., p. 96.

12 Ibid., p. 97.

13 Ibid., p. 30.

14 Ibid., p. 34.

15 Marian Sawer, 'The Soviet Image of the Commune: Lenin and beyond', in James A. Leith, ed., *Images of the Commune* (Montreal: McGill-Queen's University Press, 1978), p. 245.

16 Tartakowsky, *Nous irons chanter sur vos tombes*, p. 110.

17 See Robert Tombs, *The Paris Commune, 1871* (London: Longman, 1999) pp. 195–7.

18 Archives of Seine-Saint-Denis: 3 Mi 6 23.

19 Archives of Seine-Saint-Denis: 3 Mi 6 46 318.

20 *L'Humanité*, 7 March 1932.

21 Archives of Seine-Saint-Denis: 3 Mi 6 93 604.

22 André Marty, 'La leçon essentielle de la Commune', *Regards*, May 1933.

23 Duchet, 'Le dernier des communards', p. 29.

4 Lejeune in the USSR

1 *L'Humanité*, 3 September 1932.

2 *Monde*, 12 September 1935, p. 2.

3 Alexander Kukhno, 'Life under the Red Flag', *Literaturnaya Gazeta*, March 1967.

4 *Le Peuple*, 18 April 1940, p. 2.

5 RGASPI, 533/9/93.

6 *L'Humanité clandestine*, vol. 1 (Paris: Editions sociales, 1975), p. 353.

7 Ibid., p. 403.

8 Ibid., p. 405.

9 Ibid., p. 407.

10 Archives of the Musée de la Résistance Nationale: 85 AJ/1/1/46/1.

5 Death of a Communard

1 Duchet, 'Le dernier des communards', p. 29.

2 RGASPI, 495/195/858.

3 U. Kandeyev, 'Siberia – the Second Motherland', *Novosibirsk Evening News*, 7 January 1967.

4 Kukhno, 'Life under the Red Flag'.

5 Archives of Seine-Saint-Denis: Marty papers, Box 16, M3E.

6 *L'Humanité clandestine*, vol. 2 (Paris: Editions sociales, 1975), pp. 47–8.

7 Archives of the Musée de la Résistance Nationale: 85/AJ/1/1/20.

6 The Return of Lejeune

1 Hélène Parmelin, *La Montée au mur* (Paris: Editeurs français réunis, 1950), pp. 240–1.

2 Centre d'Histoire sociale: Marty Papers, 2-AM-11D2.

3 Archives of Seine-Saint-Denis: 2 NUM 4 9.

4 U. Mednikov, 'The Last Communard', *Ogonyok*, 13 March 1956, p. 26.

5 Alexis Truillot, 'Un enfant sous la Commune', *Europe* 374 (June 1969): 38–50.

6 Interview with the author, 19 October 2005.

7 See Marcel Picard, *Bagnolet dans l'histoire. Du franc-archer aux croquants* (Bagnolet: Société Historique de la Ville de Bagnolet, 1980), pp. 269–80.

8 Alexander Kukhno, 'Two Portraits', *Novosibirsk Evening News*, 18 March 1968.

9 Alexander Kukhno, 'Following in the footsteps of Communard Lejeune', *Soviet Siberia*, 17 March 1968.

10 Alexander Kukhno, 'When was Communard Lejeune born?' (place of publication unknown; accessed in archives of municipality of Bagnolet).

11 *L'Internationale situationniste* (Paris: Fayard, 1997), pp. 677–8.

12 Tartakowsky, *Nous irons chanter sur vos tombes*, p. 196.

13 Archives of Seine-Saint-Denis: 263 J 28.

14 Archives of Seine-Saint-Denis: decisions of PCF Politburo, BP 19710330-0527.

15 Archives of Seine-Saint-Denis: Roland Leroy papers.

16 *L'Humanité*, 18 March 1971.

17 See Hongsheng Jiang, *La Commune de Shanghai et la Commune de Paris* (Paris: La Fabrique, 2014), pp. 45–6.

18 Quoted in Alain Badiou, *The Communist Hypothesis* (London: Verso, 2010), p. 189.

19 Anon., 'A Parisian in Novosibirsk', *Soviet Siberia*, 19 March 1971.

20 *Etudes soviétiques* 276 (March 1971): 74.

21 Ibid., 81.

22 Ibid.

23 Ibid., 82.

24 Ibid.

25 Ibid., 86.

26 Archives of Seine-Saint-Denis: decisions of PCF Politburo.

27 *L'Humanité*, 24 March 1971.

28 Archives of Seine-Saint-Denis: Roland Leroy papers.

29 Archives of Seine-Saint-Denis: decisions of PCF Politburo.

30 Archives of Seine-Saint-Denis: decisions of PCF Secretariat, 2 NUM 4/9.

31 Archives of Seine-Saint-Denis: Roland Leroy papers.

32 Interview with the author, 19 October 2005.

33 Ibid.

34 *Rouge* 113 (10 May 1971): 2–3.

35 *Lutte Ouvrière* 142 (18–24 May 1971).

36 *Le Prolétaire* 104 (17–30 May 1971): 4.

37 *Le Monde libertaire* 169 (March 1971): 3.

38 Nelly Feld, 'Continuons son combat', *L'Humanité*, 24 May 1971.

39 V. Sedykh, 'At the Wall of the Communards', *Pravda*, 24 May 1971.

40 Alain Dalotel, 'La place de la Semaine Sanglante dans la commémoration du centenaire de la Commune en France', *Bulletin de la société d'histoire de la révolution de 1848 et des révolutions du XIXe siècle*, special issue (1989): 110.

41 Tartakowsky, *Nous irons chanter sur vos tombes*, p. 201.

42 *Rouge* 116 (31 May 1971): 7.

43 *Le Figaro*, 24 May 1971, p. 6.

44 Interview with the author, 8 September 2005.

7 *End of the Commune*

1 Badiou, *Communist Hypothesis*, pp. 169–70.

2 Ibid., p. 192.

3 Kristin Ross, *Communal Luxury: The Political Imaginary of the Paris Commune* (London: Verso, 2015), p. 4.

4 Interview with the author, 9 September 2005.
5 Interview with the author, 9 September 2005.
6 Jeanlouis Cornuz, *Les Caprices* (Lausanne: L'Age d'Homme, 2000), p. 224.

Select Bibliography

Primary Sources

RGASPI, Moscow

f. 495, inv. 270, file 4985 (personal file of Adrien Lejeune)
f. 517, inv. 1, file 1921 (Lejeune's autobiography and letters of
 Adela Nikolova)
f. 533, inv. 9, file 93 (Youth Communist International)
f. 533, inv. 4, file 402 (Youth Communist International)
f. 495, inv. 195, file 858 (personal file of Adela Nikolova)

Archives of the Department of Seine-Saint-Denis, Bobigny

263 J 29 (Roland Leroy papers)
B 93: 3 MI 6/23, 46, 93 (microfilms from Moscow, 1921–1939)
2 NUM 4/9 (decisions of the Secretariat of the PCF)
BP 19710330-0527 (decisions of the Politburo of the PCF)
 M3E, box 16 (André Marty papers)

Archives of the Service historique de la défense, Château de Vincennes

8/J/414 (trial of Adrien Lejeune)

National Archives, Paris

BB 24/761 (sentence of Adrien Lejeune and pleas for pardon)

Centre d'Histoire sociale, Paris

2-AM-11D2 (André Marty papers)
Archives of the Musée de la Résistance nationale, Champigny-sur-Marne
85 AJ/1/1/46/1 (clandestine publications relating to Paris Commune)

Interviews

Bertrand Beyern	09/09/2005
Marcel Cerf	09/09/2005
Jacqueline Chonavel	19/10/2005
Jean-Pierre Gast	19/10/2005
Daniel Mongeau	19/10/2005
Danielle Tartakowsky	08/09/2005

Select Bibliography

Newspapers and journals

Bulletin des Amis de la Commune de Paris
La Commune
Le Cri du peuple
Etudes soviétiques
Le Figaro
France-URSS
L'Humanité
L'Humanité clandestine
Journal officiel de la République française
Literaturnaya Gazeta
Lutte Ouvrière
Le Monde
Le Monde libertaire
Monde
Novosibirsk Evening News
Ogonyok
Le Père Duchêne
Le Peuple
Pravda
Le Prolétaire
Regards
Rouge
Soviet Siberia
La Vie Ouvrière
La Voix de l'Est

Books

Badiou, Alain, *The Communist Hypothesis* (London: Verso, 2010).

Baronnet, Jean and Chalou, Jean, *Communards en Nouvelle-Calédonie. Histoire de la déportation* (Paris: Mercure de France, 1987).

Chincholle, Charles, *Les Survivants de la Commune* (Paris: L. Boulanger, 1885).

Cornuz, Jeanlouis, *Les Désastres de la guerre* (Lausanne: L'Age d'Homme, 1994).

—, *Les Caprices* (Lausanne: L'Age d'Homme, 2000).

Courtois, Stéphane and Lazar, Marc, *Histoire du Parti communiste français* (Paris: PUF, 1995).

Duclos, Jacques, *La Commune de Paris à l'assaut du ciel* (Paris: Editions Sociales, 1971).

Gast, Jean-Pierre, *Bagnolet, 1862–1935. Un beau jour le présent s'appelle l'avenir*, (Paris: Messidor, 1988).

Jiang, Hongsheng, *La Commune de Shanghai et la Commune de Paris* (Paris: La Fabrique, 2014).

Lalouette, Jacqueline, *La libre pensée en France, 1848–1940* (Paris: Albin Michel, 2001).

Lefebvre, Henri, *La Proclamation de la Commune* (Paris: Gallimard, 1965).

Lissagaray, Prosper-Olivier, *Histoire de la Commune de 1871* (Paris: La Découverte, 2000).

Maitron, Jean, ed., *Dictionnaire biographique du mouvement ouvrier*, vol. 9 (Paris: Editions ouvrières, 1971).

Marx, Karl and Engels, Friedrich, *Writings on the Paris Commune*, edited by Hal Draper (New York: Monthly Review Press, 1971).

Mason, Edward S., *The Paris Commune: An Episode in the History of the Socialist Movement* (New York: Macmillan, 1930).

Parmelin, Hélène, *La Montée au mur* (Paris: Editeurs français réunis, 1950).

Picard, Marcel, *Bagnolet dans l'histoire. Du franc-archer aux croquants* (Bagnolet: Société Historique de la Ville de Bagnolet, 1980).

Ross, Kristin, *Communal Luxury: The Political Imaginary of the Paris Commune* (London: Verso, 2015).

Rougerie, Jacques, *La Commune de 1871* (Paris: PUF, 1988).

Rougerie, Jacques, *Le Procès des communards* (Paris: Julliard, 1978).

Tartakowsky, Danielle, *Nous irons chanter sur vos tombes. Le Père-Lachaise, XIXe–XXe siècles* (Paris: Aubier, 1999).

Tombs, Robert, *The Paris Commune, 1871* (London: Longman, 1999).

Vuillaume, Maxime, *Mes Cahiers rouges. Souvenirs de la Commune* (Paris: La Découverte, 2013).

Articles

Dalotel, Alain, 'La place de la Semaine Sanglante dans la commémoration du centenaire de la Commune en France', *Bulletin de la société d'histoire de la révolution de 1848 et des révolutions du XIXe siècle*, special issue (1989): 110.

Rebérioux, Madeleine, 'Le mur des Fédérés. Rouge, "sang craché"', in Pierre Nora, ed., *Les Lieux de mémoire*, vol. 1 (Paris: Gallimard, 1984), pp. 619–49.

Sawer, Marian, 'The Soviet Image of the Commune: Lenin and beyond', in James A. Leith, ed., *Images of the Commune* (Montreal: McGill-Queen's University Press, 1978), p. 245.

Truillot, Alexis, 'Un enfant sous la Commune', *Europe* 374 (June 1969): 38–50.